I0120290

The History of CIA's Office of Strategic Research, 1967–81

Robert Vickers

CIA History Staff

August 2019

The Center for the Study of Intelligence (CSI) was founded in 1974 in response to Director of Central Intelligence James Schlesinger's desire to create within CIA an organization that could "think through the functions of intelligence and bring the best intellects available to bear on intelligence problems." The Center, comprising both professional historians and experienced practitioners, attempts to document lessons learned from past activities, explore the needs and expectations of intelligence consumers, and stimulate serious debate on current and future intelligence challenges.

To support these efforts, CSI publishes *Studies in Intelligence* and books and monographs addressing historical, operational, doctrinal, and theoretical aspects of the intelligence profession. It also administers the CIA Museum.

Contents

The History of CIA's Office of Strategic Research, 1967–81

Organizational Acronyms and Abbreviations

ACIS	Arms Control Intelligence Staff
CIB	Current Intelligence Bulletin
CIG	Central Intelligence Group
CIWR	Current Intelligence Weekly Review
COMIREX	Committee on Imagery Requirements and Exploitation
DCI	Director of Central Intelligence
DDI	Deputy Director for Intelligence
DDO	Deputy Director for Operations
DDS&T	Deputy Director for Science and Technology
DI	Directorate of Intelligence
DO	Directorate of Operations
DS&T	Directorate of Science and Technology
FBIS	Foreign Broadcast Information Service
FMSAC	Foreign Missile and Space Analysis Center
IAS	Imagery Analysis Service
MEAC	Military-Economic Analysis Center
MEAP	Military-Economic Advisory Panel
METF	Middle East Task Force
MRA	Military-Economic Research Area
NFAC	National Foreign Assessments Center
NIB	National Intelligence Bulletin
NIC	National Intelligence Council
NID	National Intelligence Daily
NIO	National Intelligence Officer
NPIC	National Photographic Interpretation Center
OBI	Office of Basic Intelligence
OCI	Office of Current Intelligence
OCO	Office of Current Operations

Organizational Acronyms and Abbreviations, continued	
OER	Office of Economic Research
OIA	Office of Imagery Analysis
ONE	Office of National Estimates
ORPA	Office of Regional and Political Analysis
ORE	Office of Reports and Estimates
ORR	Office of Research and Reports
OSI	Office of Scientific Intelligence
OSS	Office of Strategic Studies
OWI	Office of Weapons Intelligence
PFIAB	President's Foreign Intelligence Advisory Board
SAVA	Special Assistant for Vietnam Affairs
SCAM	Strategic Cost Analysis Model
SEC	Strategic Evaluation Center
SOVA	Office of Soviet Analysis

Executive Summary

Introduction

The year 2017 marked the 50th anniversary of the creation of the Central Intelligence Agency's (CIA's) Office of Strategic Research (OSR). Director of Central Intelligence (DCI) Richard Helms established the office in July 1967 to bring together almost all the analysts in the Directorate of Intelligence (DI) responsible for military intelligence. Helms named Bruce C. Clarke Jr. to head the new office, whose mission was to provide the DCI with an independent assessment of foreign strategic military threats to US national security interests. DCI William Casey abolished OSR in October 1981 when he reorganized the DI into global regional offices rather than along functional political, economic, and military lines.[1]

During its 15 years of existence, OSR played a key role in providing in-depth military analysis and current intelligence reporting to senior policymakers on a variety of national security issues. These included the strategic military threats posed by the Soviet Bloc and Communist China, arms control measures and treaty verification, and various regional military conflicts and crises. The office grew to become one of the largest and most productive in the DI, and its leadership drew some of the Agency's best and brightest. Many of OSR's managers would subsequently hold some of the highest positions in CIA and the Intelligence Community (IC), and CIA's strategic military analysis would continue to play an important policy support role through the end of the Cold War.

The Backstory: OSR's Antecedents

Prior to the creation of OSR, CIA had gone to some lengths to avoid directly challenging the preeminent role of the Pentagon and armed services in military intelligence on the Soviet Bloc and China. That reluctance ended in the 1960s under DCIs John McCone and Richard Helms, who believed CIA had to assume the same role in military intelligence support to policymakers that it had already attained in the political and economic realms. CIA was created by the National Security Act of 1947, which also created the Office of the Secretary of Defense and the National Security Council (NSC). The NSC's role was to coordinate national security and foreign policy on behalf of the president with the various government agencies involved, including the Departments of State and Defense as well as the armed services and CIA. One of the NSC's first acts was to delineate the primary intelligence responsibilities of each agency. State was charged with collecting and analyzing political and social intelligence; the various armed services were responsible for military intelligence; and CIA produced economic, scientific, and technical intelligence.[2]

President Harry Truman selected R.Adm. Roscoe Hillenkoetter, the head of the Central Intelligence Group (CIG), as CIA's first director. The CIG was the follow-on organization to the wartime Office of Strategic Services (OSS). CIA inherited a staff of about 300 analysts from the CIG, sufficient for it to be an independent producer of intelligence. Organized in the Office of Reports and Estimates (ORE), the staff had a broad range of research, current reporting, and estimating responsibilities, primarily on economic, scientific, and technical issues. In late 1948, DCI Hillenkoetter created the Office of Scientific Intelligence (OSI) to focus on analysis of Soviet Bloc scientific and technical issues.

The outbreak of the Korean War in June 1950 created new demands on CIA for additional current reporting on the situation as well as more in-depth analysis. In October 1950, Truman replaced Hillenkoetter, who was blamed for a perceived CIA failure to warn of the outbreak of hostilities, with General Walter Bedell Smith. DCI Smith had wartime experience as an intelligence consumer while serving as General Dwight Eisenhower's Chief of Staff, and he was the US Ambassador to the Soviet Union from 1946 to 1949. Smith was convinced that the Soviet strategic threat was enduring, and he had strong ideas about what he wanted in an intelligence organization. In late 1950, DCI Smith abolished ORE and created three new intelligence components to cover the broad spectrum of intelligence products CIA was preparing. The Office of Research and Reports (ORR) was responsible for in-depth analysis, the Office of Current Intelligence (OCI) did daily reporting, and the Office of National Estimates (ONE) produced integrated national intelligence estimates.

DCI Smith soon picked a noted economist from the Massachusetts Institute of Technology (MIT), Max Millikan, to be the new head of ORR. In theory, ORR was created to address Soviet Bloc economic intelligence. Millikan, however, had been a member of the OSS intelligence staff during World War II, and he strongly believed that the strength of a nation's economy was key to its capability to wage war. Thus, he organized ORR so that it could analyze all aspects of the Soviet economy—including the size and cost of the defense sector—in depth. To do so, Millikan created four economic divisions: industrial, materials, economic services, and economic analysis. His goal was to estimate the potential Soviet Bloc strategic threat by looking closely at the various sectors of the economy, particularly those that contributed to Soviet military power. He believed that this micro-analytic approach would help analysts to estimate the total economic resources available to the Soviet Bloc, the allocation of these resources to the military sector, and the strengths and limitations of the economy. This in turn would assist in determining enemy capabilities and weaknesses and help policymakers exploit Soviet Bloc economic vulnerabilities. Millikan also wanted ORR to make independent evaluations of military service estimates of Soviet military production in support of its defense spending analysis despite the bureaucratic obstacles to getting consistent and reliable data from the Department of Defense (DoD).

A large analytic workforce was required to do the minute inspection and costing of each facet of the Soviet economy. ORR grew rapidly during its first few years, primarily in the four economic divisions that covered the Soviet Bloc economies and Communist China. These divisions alone grew from about 150 personnel to nearly 500 by 1953. A key unit of the four was the Industrial Division, which had branches that focused on major military and civilian production sectors, including aircraft, ships, weapons, ammunition, and electronics. A key problem, however, was the lack of detailed information on the Soviet economy and defense spending. These details were treated as state secrets by the Soviet government; the little data that Moscow released was regarded by CIA as either inadequate or deceptive.

DCI Smith created the Directorate of Intelligence (DI) in January 1952 to manage all of CIA's analytic components, including ORR, OCI, ONE, and OSI. Millikan left CIA soon after to return to MIT, and he was succeeded as head of ORR by Robert Amory. A former Harvard Law School professor, Amory wanted ORR to not only be able to check DoD estimates of Soviet military production, but to do its own independent assessments. Loftus Becker, whom DCI Smith had picked to head the newly created DI, objected. Becker was concerned about CIA encroachment on service intelligence responsibilities, and he was opposed to CIA doing its own analysis of Soviet weapons production.

During this period, Amory made support of National Intelligence Estimates (NIEs) a high priority for ORR. A procedure was developed to produce detailed contributions to estimates on the Soviet economy and Soviet defense spending. Walter Langer, the first head of ONE, had been succeeded in January 1952 by the renowned Sherman Kent, who was to remain in this position until 1967. ORR made major contributions to the first two estimates on Soviet Bloc military capabilities, completed in 1952 and 1953.[3] The contributions were noteworthy in that the Industrial Division provided production estimates and projections for Soviet Bloc fighters, bombers, cruisers, destroyers, and submarines. At Becker's insistence, however, Amory had to ensure that the weapons production estimates were based on production data provided by the armed services to ORR.

In 1953, significant changes took place in CIA's and ORR's leadership that would last for the rest of the decade. In February 1953, DCI Smith left CIA to become Under Secretary of State; newly elected President Dwight Eisenhower replaced Smith with Allen Dulles, the deputy DCI. Dulles was another OSS veteran; he had joined CIA in early 1951 as the first deputy director for plans and had become deputy DCI in August 1951. In April 1953, Dulles replaced Becker as the deputy director for intelligence (DDI) with Amory, who held this post for the next nine years. Amory was in turn replaced as head of ORR by Otto Guthe, a geographer from the University of Michigan, who held the position until 1965.

In contrast to Becker, Amory encouraged ORR to expand the scope of its military-economic research activities. In June 1953, Guthe reorganized ORR into three major units: the Geographic Research Area, the Coordination Area, and the Economic Research Area (ERA). Guthe then picked Edward Allen, an economist from American University, to head ERA, which included all four of the economic divisions. Allen promptly did a comprehensive review of the research program and began to make ERA an all-source operation inside a special communications intelligence (COMINT) center. To do so, he abolished the Strategic Division, which had been established as ORR's COMINT cell, and moved its personnel inside ERA. He also created a new Military Economics Branch inside the Economic Analysis Division. Allen wanted ERA to estimate the Soviet Union's gross national product, including doing estimates of each sector of the economy. The Military Economic Branch was to provide an estimate of the cost of the military sector, a new responsibility for ORR that had significant long-term consequences.

The efforts by Smith, Millikan, Amory, and Guthe in the early 1950s to build a strong military-economic analytic capability in CIA that focused on the Soviet Bloc strategic military threat to the United States had a lasting legacy. Those efforts directly contributed to eventually enabling CIA to do its own independent estimates of Soviet military production and to effectively challenge the military force estimates of the US military services. This led to the creation of OSR in the late 1960s. The path to its creation was not easy, however, and the period was marked by continued controversy between CIA and DoD over the full extent of the Soviet military threat. These differences eventually spilled into the political and policymaking arenas.

Key Sources

This study will examine in more detail how CIA's growing capability to do independent analysis of the Soviet military threat led to major disagreements with the US armed services over Soviet military capabilities and intentions, beginning in the Dulles era. Much has already been written about these controversies and how they played out. This history will focus primarily on the role that key CIA leaders and managers played in the development of the Agency's military analytic capabilities, rather than on the controversies themselves. It will also provide detailed information on how OSR was formed and on those individuals who contributed heavily to its success. Many of the early details are derived from two draft studies of the history of CIA's military analysis. The first is "The Development of Strategic Analysis at CIA, 1947-1967" by two former senior OSR officers, Leonard F. Parkinson and Logan H. Potter.[4] A draft was completed in 1974 but never published. The second is "Strategic Military Analysis in CIA" by Donald P. Steury, a former member of CIA's History Staff. Steury's draft was completed in 1994 and was also never published.[5] It covers the period from 1947 through the demise of OSR in 1981.

Another major source for this study is a book by two former senior managers in CIA, Noel E. Firth, who served as acting director of OSR in the mid-1970s, and James H. Noren, who spent almost his entire 32-year career at CIA doing research and analysis of the Soviet economy. Their book, titled *Soviet Defense Spending: A History of CIA Estimates, 1950-1990*, provides an in-depth look at how CIA developed its capability to do independent estimates of Soviet defense spending and how this led to the creation of OSR's ability to do comprehensive assessments of Soviet Bloc strategic and conventional forces along with analysis of Soviet military capabilities and intentions.[6]

Three books by former CIA senior managers also offer useful insights on intelligence analysis in CIA. These include *The Unknown CIA: My Three Decades with the Agency*, by former DDI R. Jack Smith, which includes a discussion of the formation and early years of OSR.[7] A second such book is *Secrecy and Democracy: The CIA in Transition*, by former DCI Stansfield Turner.[8] Turner gives high praise to CIA's military analysis and faults the military intelligence agencies for their tendency to exaggerate the enemy threat.

Another valuable source is *From the Shadows: The Ultimate Insider's Story of Five Presidents and How They Won the Cold War* by former DCI Robert M. Gates.[9] Gates discusses in detail the key role that CIA played in providing intelligence support, including military analysis, to five presidents from Richard Nixon through George Bush. Finally, *Casey: From the OSS to the CIA*, by Joseph Persico, provides much detail on Casey's early years as DCI, including the abolition of OSR and the reorganization of the DI.[10]

Recorded and personal interviews with former senior managers in CIA, especially those who served in OSR, provided another key source of information for this history. In addition to Firth, these include former DDCI Richard Kerr and former CIA Executive Director Robert "Rae" Huffstutler.[11] A theme of these interviews is the persistent struggle during the Cold War era between CIA and DoD over their different assessments of Soviet military capabilities and intentions. Kerr and Huffstutler note that the mission of the US armed services is to win wars, and that it is both prudent and understandable for the Pentagon to lean toward a worst-case assessment of the Soviet military threat. The former OSR managers strongly believe, however, that CIA needed to challenge DoD with its own independent assessments of foreign military threats in order to better serve US presidents and other senior policymakers.

A final major source of information was the wealth of declassified CIA estimates and other analytic products that CIA, including OSR, produced on the Soviet Union and Soviet Bloc military capabilities. These are available on-line at www.cia.gov, and they include several publications done by CIA's Center for the Study of Intelligence (CSI). One is a compendium of NIEs on Soviet strategic forces titled *Intentions and Capabilities: Estimates of Soviet Forces, 1950–1983.*[12] Another focuses on Soviet Bloc conventional forces and is titled *CIA Analysis of Warsaw Pact Forces: The Importance of Clandestine Reporting, 1955–1985.*[13] A third, titled *Watching the Bear: Essays on CIA's Analysis of the Soviet Union*, includes a chapter on CIA's military analysis.[14] A final source is *CIA's Analysis of the Soviet Union, 1947–1991*, which includes a chapter on NIEs on Soviet military intentions and capabilities during the Cold War era.[15]

Chapter Summaries

The ***first chapter*** of this history of OSR examines the Dulles era and the key people involved in the growing capability of ORR to do independent Soviet military force assessments. This capability grew out of CIA's efforts to use a building-block approach to better define the Soviet defense budget, partially by attempting to more precisely estimate the cost of Soviet weapons production. Dulles initially believed strongly that the military services had been given the authority to produce military intelligence for policymakers and that CIA should not challenge the results of such efforts. He changed his view with the advent of the so-called bomber- and missile-gap controversies in the late 1950s. The controversies were not fully resolved until the development of new satellite photographic collection capabilities in the early 1960s led to more accurate assessments of Soviet strategic forces.

Chapter two focuses on the significant growth of CIA's capability to do strategic military analysis in the early 1960s during the tenure of DCI John McCone. President John F. Kennedy appointed McCone to replace Allen Dulles in November 1961 in the wake of the Bay of Pigs debacle. Unlike Dulles, McCone believed strongly that CIA needed to do its own independent analysis and make key judgments on a wide range of topics, including strategic military intelligence, without having to rely on input from DoD. In the wake of the Cuban Missile Crisis in late 1962, McCone also argued that CIA needed to be informed about what was happening in defense policy so the DCI could provide President Kennedy with the kinds of intelligence support he expected. As a result, under McCone, CIA's support to national policymakers became more frequent and direct, and such interactions were no longer tied primarily to NIEs.

McCone's approach to military intelligence analysis fit in well with the expectations of new Secretary of Defense Robert S. McNamara. McNamara believed that effective management of DoD's budget required extensive program planning supported by detailed analysis of various alternatives. This management approach also required a five-year projection of US defense needs for complete weapons and equipment systems and their dollar costs. McNamara wanted to apply this same systems analysis to future NIEs on Soviet Bloc military capabilities. This involved examining the Soviet threat in separate weapons system categories: strategic offensive, strategic defensive, and general purpose forces. McNamara also wanted five-year Soviet military force projections, consideration of likely alternatives, and analysis of Soviet military expenditures in rubles.

As a result, McNamara placed new demands on CIA for more detailed analyses of Soviet Bloc weapons systems and associated economic costs. DoD and the newly created Defense Intelligence Agency (DIA) were unable to provide such data. Moreover, the advent of satellite photography in 1961 gave CIA the ability to greatly reduce longstanding uncertainties about Soviet strategic and conventional force levels and weapon systems, as well as identify military production and research and development facilities. Under McCone, organizational changes soon followed. Ray Cline, who formerly served in OCI, replaced Robert Amory as the DDI in May 1962. ORR then consolidated military research in a new Military-Economic Research Division headed by Edward Proctor. Finally, R. Jack Smith, who had replaced Huntington Sheldon as head of OCI in April 1962, restructured OCI's Military Division along mission and functional lines under the leadership of Bruce Clarke. Smith, Proctor, and Clarke represented a new generation of DI senior managers under McCone, and all would eventually become DDIs.

The Cuban Missile Crisis in late 1962 represented a significant intelligence success for McCone and his new senior DI leadership team in providing detailed military intelligence support to the president and senior policymakers. As a result, CIA's intelligence support to Pentagon planners began to expand dramatically, and CIA also began to provide Soviet intelligence analysis to the Arms Control and Disarmament Agency (ACDA). China's strategic weapons programs got new attention, as did Soviet ground forces. These efforts required closer interaction between CIA and the newly formed DIA, and conflicts began to develop between the two organizations over roles and responsibilities. Finally, the process for producing NIEs on Soviet strategic military forces began to change significantly as a result of the new DoD requirements for more comprehensive analysis of the Soviet military establishment.

All these developments created new pressures for consolidating military research in CIA in a single organization. McCone had resigned as DCI in April 1965 and was replaced briefly by Admiral William Raborn and then by Richard Helms in June 1966. Ray Cline had been replaced as DDI by R. Jack Smith in early 1966, and Smith selected Ed Proctor as his deputy. Smith and Proctor were determined to create a single military analytic organization in the DI, and Smith appointed Bruce Clarke to study how this could be best accomplished. By this time, OSI had been put in the newly formed Directorate of Science and Technology (DS&T), created in August 1963 under Albert "Bud" Wheelon. Smith had moved ONE out of the DI and placed it directly under the DCI in January 1966. Sherman Kent then retired as head of ONE in late 1967; he was replaced with Abbot E. Smith in early 1968.

Clarke formed a small team to lay out the justification for the new office and do detailed organizational planning. The result was a completed report to the DDI in late 1966, and a final memorandum of recommendation was sent to DCI Helms in late June 1967. Clarke made clear that the purpose of the new office was to "describe, measure and forecast the weight of a country's military capabilities…on its national goals and foreign policy objectives, particularly as they affect the national security interests of the United States. To do this requires an appreciation of the political purposes for which military forces and programs exist. But more than that, it requires an understanding of the military forces…themselves."[16] Helms quickly approved, and OSR was officially established on 1 July 1967 with Clarke as its first director and Roland Inlow as his deputy. The new office was given the name Strategic Research rather than "military research" to avoid directly challenging the intelligence prerogatives of DIA and the military services.

Chapter three concentrates on the first few years of OSR under Clarke and the early challenges to the new office, including the Soviet invasion of Czechoslovakia and the change in administrations from President Lyndon Johnson to President Richard Nixon. It also examines the major components and senior leadership of OSR and the roles they played in military intelligence support to policymakers. A subtheme will be the increasing tensions between OSR and the various intelligence components in DoD, including the armed services and DIA. The sources for this chapter are mainly interviews with former senior CIA officials as well as organizational charts and annual reports that Clarke did for the DDI.[17]

The leadership of OSR at its creation consisted of managers and personnel drawn primarily from the former Military Division in OCI, which Clarke had headed, and from the Military-Economic Research Area of ORR, which Inlow had run. To this DDI Smith added the military branch of the China Division in OCI. The geographic focus of the new office was primarily on the Soviet Union, Communist China, and other communist states except Vietnam. Smith left analysis and reporting on the war in Vietnam to the newly created Office of Economic Research (OER), which contained the remaining economic research elements of the former ORR. This was done for analytic continuity and to avoid involving OSR in the political controversies surrounding the Vietnam conflict.

OSR was able to hit the ground running because its structure was based largely on the previously existing components from ORR and OCI. It had a front office with several staff elements, the Factory Markings Staff, and four large divisions. The Programs Analysis Division did military-economic research and had three branches: Cost Analysis, Military Expenditures, and Strategy and Trends. The Strategic Forces Division, which focused primarily on the Soviet Union, contained three branches: Defensive Missiles, Offensive Missiles, and Space Systems. The Theater Forces Division had four branches: Naval Systems, Aircraft Systems, Ground Forces, and China. The Regional Analysis Division did current intelligence reporting and had three branches: USSR/Eastern Europe, China/Far East, and a small general branch later renamed the Free World Branch. About 180 people, most of them from the former ORR, staffed the new office.[18]

The advent of the Nixon administration in early 1969 created a whole new set of demands for military intelligence support, which OSR strove mightily to provide. The focus of the Johnson administration had been on analysis of the capabilities of the communist military forces confronting the United States in support of defense planning. The new administration, with Henry Kissinger as Assistant to the President for National Security Affairs, required detailed military intelligence input on a wide variety of issues in support of broader national security policy planning, including arms control negotiations for both strategic and conventional forces and growing concerns about the Chinese military threat and the expansion of the Cold War in the Third World.

To manage the effort of overseeing national security policy on matters pertaining to military policy decisionmaking, Kissinger created several new mechanisms. The first was the National Security Study Memorandum (NSSM) process, which involved detailed analysis of the military threats to US strategic interests in various regions of the world and the appropriate US force posture in response. Another policy mechanism was the Defense Policy Review Committee (DPRC), created to undertake detailed studies of US defense programs and future force levels. In addition, Kissinger created intelligence verification panels to support the new Strategic Arms Limitation Talks (SALT) and the Mutual and Balanced Force Reduction (MBFR) negotiations with the Soviet Union.

OSR worked hard to meet these new intelligence demands. Kissinger was a difficult customer, as was Secretary of Defense Melvin Laird. Neither accepted CIA military intelligence assessments on the Soviet Bloc at face value. Kissinger had a vast interest and knowledge of Soviet affairs and wanted intelligence inputs that separated facts and opinion, presumably so he and the president could draw their own conclusions. He also wanted not just intelligence judgments but the reasoning behind them, and he wanted key strategic military estimates to include alternative assumptions, opinions, and force projections.

The first significant intelligence clash that CIA had with the Nixon administration occurred in early 1969 over the annual update to the NIE done the previous year on Soviet strategic attack forces.[19, 20] CIA analysts in OSR and the DS&T differed with the Air Force over whether the latest Soviet intercontinental ballistic missile (ICBM), the SS-9, had the capability to carry multiple independently targetable re-entry vehicles (MIRVs). Both agreed that the missile could carry three warheads, but the Air Force assessed that the missiles were MIRVs, while CIA did not. Kissinger and Laird supported the Air Force position and argued that the Soviets were striving for a first-strike capability. To counter such a capability, Laird publicly supported the need for a greatly expanded US anti-ballistic missile system, and Kissinger used the assessment to support the need for a SALT treaty with Moscow. When CIA continued to disagree, Kissinger accused it of bias and ordered an independent assessment of all the evidence so the NSC staff could draw its own conclusions. The CIA position was eventually vindicated, but this was only the first of major differences that the Agency would have with the Nixon administration over strategic military intelligence analysis.

Chapter four examines in more detail the last three years of Bruce Clarke's tenure as director of OSR, from mid-1970 until mid-1973. The decade of the 1970s was the age of detente, and OSR was called upon to provide considerable intelligence support to senior policy officials. To meet the growing requirements of the Nixon administration, OSR relied heavily on signals intelligence (SIGINT) input from the National Security Agency (NSA), created in 1952 as part of DoD, and on imagery input from the National Photographic Interpretation Center (NPIC), created in 1961 by CIA and placed in the DI. OSR also received imagery input from the DI's Imagery Analysis Service (IAS), which was created in early 1967 to provide direct imagery support to CIA. OSR also worked closely with the DS&T's Office of Scientific Intelligence (OSI) and its Foreign Missile and Space Analysis Center (FMSAC). FMSAC had been created by DCI McCone in November 1963 under Carl Duckett to provide space and missile intelligence and expertise to both CIA and DoD.

OSR began providing more detailed information to ONE for new NIEs on Soviet and Chinese military forces and capabilities. The 1969 NIE on Soviet strategic forces had been heavily criticized by the Nixon White House for lacking adequate intelligence input. A new format was established for the 1970 Soviet strategic forces NIE, which contained much more detailed intelligence and alternative outcomes. At the same time, DCI Helms made a decision to involve OSR, OSI, and FMSAC more directly in drafting a CIA team's contribution to Soviet military estimates. As a result of these changes, a much more comprehensive NIE was issued in early 1971. President Nixon then sent a note to DCI Helms commending him and the entire IC for producing a "particularly useful" estimate.[21]

On 1 July 1972, OSR celebrated its fifth anniversary. Although Helms was not able to attend the event, he sent a brief letter of congratulations. In it, Helms wrote, "You have come a long way in the past five years... Your voice is heard throughout the government where national security matters are discussed. Your views are respected and your analysis is used with confidence."[22] During this period, the office had grown to over 200 personnel and Clarke had added a special assistant to the director for strategic arms talks to oversee joint DI-DS&T support to the SALT negotiations. He also combined the former Strategic and Theater Divisions into a new, large Soviet and Eastern European Forces Division and added a smaller Asian Communist Forces Division to meet growing demands from the Nixon administration for strategic intelligence on China and North Korea. The Programs Analysis Division, which did strategic evaluations, planning and costing, and technical analysis, had continued to expand and had become the second largest division in OSR. The Regional Analysis Division, which did current reporting, remained the smallest division. Finally, the Factory Markings Staff was disestablished in June 1972, and DIA was given the responsibility for creating a Joint Factory Markings Center.[23]

Little did Clarke know that major changes in CIA were about to take place during the next year, resulting in his departure the following September. In November 1972, newly re-elected President Nixon asked DCI Helms to resign and become US Ambassador to Iran. Nixon replaced Helms in January 1973 with James Schlesinger, who had been assistant director of the Bureau of the Budget and then head of the Atomic Energy Commission. Nixon gave Schlesinger a mandate to shake up CIA and reduce its personnel, and Schlesinger wasted little time in doing so. Most of the DCI's changes were aimed at reducing the size and influence of the clandestine service, which he renamed the Directorate of Operations (DO). Schlesinger greatly strengthened the DS&T by merging FMSAC and OSI's Defensive Systems Division into a new Office of Weapons Intelligence (OWI) responsible for technical analysis of both offensive and defensive weapons systems. Schlesinger also moved NPIC into the DS&T from the DI in May 1973.

Clarke knew Schlesinger from Schlesinger's days as assistant budget director, when Clarke had provided him with strategic briefings. He found Schlesinger a challenging customer but got along well with him and supported his efforts to improve the NIE process to better meet policymakers' needs. In particular, Schlesinger wanted NIEs to address not just the "what" but the "why," and OSR responded accordingly. During Schlesinger's tenure, Clarke oversaw the establishment of a new Military-Economic Advisory Panel (MEAP) of economic experts from outside the government to review OSR's analysis of Soviet defense spending. Helms had previously approved the creation of the panel at DDI Proctor's recommendation in 1972 in response to DIA's increased criticism of OSR's cost analysis. It took a full year to recruit and clear the panel members for access to classified intelligence, and the MEAP met for the first time in April 1973. Although the first MEAP report issued in July 1974 generally supported CIA's Soviet defense costing efforts, DIA's criticism was only the beginning of a long series of DoD and other outside challenges to CIA's defense costing efforts that would last the next two decades.[24]

Nixon announced suddenly in May 1973 that he was making Schlesinger his new Secretary of Defense and replacing him with William Colby, who was then CIA's deputy director for operations (DDO). The change took place in September 1973; soon after, Clarke left OSR at Schlesinger's request to become DoD's representative to the MBFR talks in Vienna. One of Clarke's last official acts was to create a new Strategic Evaluation Center (SEC) in OSR at Schlesinger's request to do integrated analysis of the national security policy of the Soviet Union and other key foreign countries and to provide net force assessments to the NSC staff.[25] The SEC was originally headed by Fritz Ermarth, whom Schlesinger had brought to his staff from RAND, but it was later briefly run by Robert Gates, who later became DCI and subsequently Secretary of Defense.

Clarke's departure from OSR was the end of a seven-year era of sustained strong leadership for the office. Many of those who worked for Clarke during that time regard him as one of the best CIA mentors they ever knew, both in substance and personnel management. What was to be Clarke's one-year assignment in Vienna lasted until 1978. By then, DCI Colby had abolished ONE in late 1973 and replaced it with individual national intelligence officers (NIOs) who reported to a new deputy to the DCI for national intelligence. DCI Stansfield Turner subsequently created the National Foreign Assessments Center

OSR Directors

Bruce C. Clarke Jr.
July 1967-September 1973

E. Henry "Hank" Knoche
September 1973-June 1975

Richard L. Lehman
June 1975-February 1976

Noel E. Firth
February 1976-November 1976

Sidney N. Graybeal
November 1976-January 1979

Robert M. "Rae" Huffstutler
January 1970-October 1981

(NFAC) in October 1977 by combining the DI and the NIOs under a single leader. Turner then appointed Robert Bowie as the first director of NFAC. Meanwhile, Bruce Clarke, after brief stints at the Pentagon under Secretary of Defense Harold Brown and at the Department of Energy under Secretary Schlesinger, joined Bowie's staff at NFAC in early 1979. When Bowie retired in August 1969, Turner replaced him with Clarke. As a result, Clarke was once again overseeing OSR (see chapter eight for discussion).

During OSR's last eight years, it continued to provide strong military intelligence support to national security policymakers and to arms control negotiations and treaty verification efforts. However, it also came under powerful attack from both Congress and critics inside and outside the government who believed OSR was underestimating the strategic military threat posed by the Soviet Union. Until its demise in October 1981, OSR had four different directors and one acting director. Three of the new directors—E. Henry "Hank" Knoche, Richard Lehman, and Sidney Graybeal—were experienced CIA managers who had previously held senior intelligence positions. The acting director, Noel Firth, and OSR's last director, Rae Huffstutler, were former DDI analysts who had joined OSR at its creation and risen through the ranks.

These five heads of OSR served under four presidents—Richard Nixon, Gerald Ford, Jimmy Carter, and Ronald Reagan—and under four

DCIs—Colby, Bush, Turner, and Casey. All went on to more senior positions in CIA. Knoche became the deputy DCI under George H. W. Bush in 1976. Lehman served as the deputy to the DCI for national intelligence under Bush and then was named chairman of the National Intelligence Council (NIC) when Turner formed the NIC in December 1979. Firth was named the first director of the Office of Imagery Analysis (OIA), the former IAS, in 1977. Huffstutler was named the director of the new Office of Soviet Analysis (SOVA) in the DI after OSR was abolished in 1981, then became the director of NPIC in 1984, deputy director for administration in 1988, and finally the executive director of CIA in 1992. After Graybeal retired from CIA in 1979, he was appointed to the Defense Policy Board.

Chapter five focuses on the period from September 1973 to June 1975 when Knoche was designated D/OSR. Knoche had had a long career in CIA beginning in 1953 when he transferred from NSA. He subsequently joined DCI McCone's executive staff in 1962 and remained on the DCI staff under Raborn and Helms. He then became executive director of NPIC from 1967 to 1969 and worked on the DCI Planning, Programming and Budget staff from 1969 to 1970. He was DD/OCI until March 1972, when he became director of the Foreign Broadcast Information Service (FBIS). Knoche said he was surprised when DDI Proctor picked him to head OSR, but he took the job willingly.[26]

Knoche arrived in OSR at a very busy time for the office. In October 1973, a major war broke out when Egypt and Syria launched a surprise attack on Israel, and OSR became heavily involved in monitoring the conflict. John Paisley was already in place as deputy director; Knoche initially relied on Paisley to help him run the office. Paisley had a strong background doing military cost analysis for both ORR and OSR, and Clarke had made him his deputy when Roland Inlow retired. Paisley decided to retire in early 1974, however, and Knoche appointed Noel Firth, who had just returned from the National War College, as his acting deputy director in July 1974.[27] Soon thereafter, DCI Colby asked Knoche to help investigate a special intelligence collection program. In December 1974, Seymour Hersh published his famous *New York Times* article on CIA's history of rogue operations, which led to President Ford's creation of the Rockefeller Commission to investigate alleged CIA misdeeds. In January 1975, Colby appointed Knoche as his special assistant to coordinate the CIA response to the commission's recommendations and subsequent congressional investigations. As a result, Firth ended up running OSR until Richard Lehman took over in June 1975.

One of Knoche's first official acts as D/OSR was to announce a reorganization that created two new divisions: the Soviet Strategic Forces Division to focus on SALT support and the Warsaw Pact-NATO Division (soon renamed Theater Forces Division) to address MBFR issues. Clarke had planned this reorganization before he left for Vienna to join the MBFR negotiations. A new Asian Programs Branch was also created in the Eastern Forces Division to expand OSR's analysis of Chinese military strategy and doctrine and do research on regional military forces.[28] Clarke thus left Knoche with an expanded office and a strong new team of experienced managers who served him well during his extended absences in the DCI front office.

Chapter six examines the period from June 1975 until February 1976 when Lehman was head of OSR, as well as the period from February to November 1976 when Firth was acting director. During this time, Colby continued to be besieged by the investigations of the Church and Pike Committees. Soon after Lehman arrived in OSR, Colby asked him to join a group of senior CIA mangers to study CIA's future, particularly the DCI's relationship with the secretary of defense, to preempt a congressional inquiry. Lehman ended up drafting the report, which Colby praised.[29] Although the paper was never published, Lehman became a de facto special assistant to Colby dealing with congressional relations. As a result, he never returned to OSR, and Noel Firth ran the office unofficially beginning in mid-1975. In January 1976, President Ford replaced Colby as DCI with George H. W. Bush. Firth was then officially appointed acting D/OSR, a post he held until November 1976, when he left to become the first director of OIA.

Firth had a background in CIA and OSR as a military costing expert, which served him well during his tenure as acting director. In early 1976, CIA announced that it had completed a major upward revision in its ruble estimate of Soviet military spending during the 1970-75 period. Not only was the Soviet defense budget significantly larger than previously estimated, but so was the percentage of Soviet GNP absorbed by defense. The revision had been done jointly by a team of OSR and OER analysts based on new ruble price and cost data rather than the discovery of new Soviet defense programs. Firth makes a strong defense of the revised spending estimate in his book on the subject, but he acknowledges that the shock of the abrupt change created a deep and lasting skepticism among many in the policy and intelligence communities, as well as in academia, about the accuracy of CIA's former and subsequent analysis of the Soviet defense spending. Nevertheless, CIA's military spending analysis of the Soviet Union continued in support of DoD budget deliberations until the end of the Cold War.[30]

The upward revision of Soviet defense spending came at a time when the President's Foreign Intelligence Advisory Board (PFIAB) was challenging the accuracy of all CIA Soviet strategic intelligence estimates produced during the previous 10 years. PFIAB consisted of 12 prominent members drawn from outside the Intelligence Community (IC) and selected by the President. In May 1976, DCI Bush agreed to a PFIAB request that the next Soviet strategic estimate be done using competitive analysis from two teams: A Team, composed of IC analysts, and B Team, composed of outside experts. Three key issues were to be addressed by separate A and B teams—two technical and one political—on Soviet strategic objectives. The new NIO for strategic programs, Howard Stoertz, and the former deputy director of OSR, John Paisley, oversaw the effort. The competitive analysis on Soviet strategic objectives was by far the most contentious. The B Team effort was led by a conservative Harvard professor, Richard Pipes; its final report, issued in December 1976, challenged the whole series of CIA Soviet strategic estimates for characterizing Soviet strategic intentions as defensive rather than offensive in nature.[31]

By the time that the B Team's report was issued, Sayre Stevens had replaced Ed Proctor as DDI in June 1976. Stevens had a strong technical background in the DS&T and had been Carl Duckett's deputy from January 1974 until May 1976. When Duckett retired as DDS&T, he was replaced by Les Dirks in June 1976, and Stevens got Proctor's job. Stevens then appointed Graybeal as head of OSR with Firth as his deputy in November 1976. Graybeal came to OSR with a strong technical background and as an arms control negotiator with the State Department, and he was a logical choice to oversee OSR's continued contributions to the SALT and MBFR negotiations. The deputy director to the DCI for national intelligence, Richard Lehman, and Graybeal both criticized the B Team's report as based not on intelligence but on the long-held political views of some of its members. DCI Bush agreed, noting that the competitive analysis effort had contributed little to the analytic judgments of the 1976 NIE on Soviet strategic forces.[32]

Chapter seven discusses the period from November 1976 to January 1979 when Graybeal was head of OSR. Soon after Graybeal became D/OSR, President Jimmy Carter took office and replaced DCI Bush with Admiral Turner. During Graybeal's tenure, OSR continued to provide extensive arms control intelligence support to the Carter administration and to contribute to key military NIEs. Stevens encouraged OSR to work more closely with OSI and OWI. Both OSI and OWI had been transferred from the DS&T to the DI in November 1976, and Evans Hineman, who had been D/OWI prior to the transfer, remained as its head. Rae Huffstutler, who had been the head of OSR's Theater Forces Division, was then sent to OWI as Hineman's deputy to help enhance cooperation between the two offices.

In April 1977, Graybeal reorganized OSR and created a new Military–Economic Analysis Center (MEAC) to strengthen its research on Soviet and other communist military programs, including doing cost analysis of Chinese defense spending. This was done in the wake of the A-Team/B-Team exercise and the criticism of OSR's assessments of Soviet defense spending. Graybeal also made some changes to several of the other divisions and to the Strategic Evaluation Center to reflect a new emphasis on force effectiveness and on military policy and doctrine. One goal was for OSR to provide better support for special projects done jointly with other DI offices. Meanwhile, OSR continued to contribute heavily to NIEs on Soviet strategic capabilities and Soviet global goals and intentions.[33]

Chapter eight focuses on the period from January 1979 to January 1981 when Carter was still President and Turner was still DCI. In late 1978, Graybeal decided to retire, and Huffstutler replaced him in early 1979. Huffstutler had a long background as a military and technical analyst, first in ORR and then in OSR and OWI. He had strong support for the position from new Associate Deputy Director for Intelligence

(ADDI) Stevens—he had worked with Stevens before on SALT support—and from Hineman, who still headed OWI. Huffstutler inherited an office that soon became the largest in the DI and that continued to contribute significantly to the SALT and MBFR negotiations and to various military NIEs.

Meanwhile, Clarke had been appointed the D/NFAC by Turner in August 1979; John Hicks was in place as his deputy. Hicks had headed NPIC from 1973 to 1978 and had become Bowie's deputy in early 1979. Clarke had developed a close relationship with Turner while D/OSR, and with DCI approval, he soon made two major organizational changes in NFAC. One was to merge OSI and OWI into the Office of Scientific and Weapons Research (OSWR) in early 1980 with Wayne Boring as its director. Another was to put all the NIOs into a new organization, the National Intelligence Council (NIC), in late 1979 with Richard Lehman as its chairman. Clarke believed that the NIOs needed a strong organizational structure and firm leadership in order to function as a corporate Intelligence Community body.[34]

Turner took a strong interest in NIEs and believed that as DCI, he had the right to express his own views rather than simply reflect the views of the various intelligence agencies. Turner and Clarke also both believed that CIA should have a stronger independent voice in the estimative process, primarily because it was less influenced by policy bias and could be more objective in its analysis. In the 1979 NIE on Soviet strategic capabilities for nuclear conflict, Turner expressed his support of the CIA judgment that the Soviet Union had not achieved enough strategic military superiority for its leaders to risk provoking a nuclear conflict with the United States.[35] DIA and the military intelligences services strongly objected. As a result, the 1980 NIE on the same topic contained two sets of key judgments, one representing the DCI and CIA and the other DIA and the military services. The latter argued that CIA analysis was based on a net assessment of Soviet and US capabilities that was not a proper function of an intelligence agency. As DCI, Turner rebutted this position, stating that he did not believe that it was in the national interest for DoD to control all comparisons of US and opposing military forces.[36]

Meanwhile, soon after Clarke became D/NFAC, Huffstutler and OSR began a major research paper on the development of Soviet military power since the fall of Khrushchev. This was to be an in-depth project that would be ready in time for the next presidential administration. The final product, titled *The Development of Soviet Military Power: Trends Since 1965 and Prospects for the 1980s,* took two years to prepare and drew on inputs from every office in NFAC. It was a comprehensive survey that took into account political, economic, and technical factors as well as military ones and was more deeply researched and balanced than then current national intelligence estimates. By the time that it was issued in April 1981, Ronald Reagan had assumed office and William Casey had become DCI.[37]

Chapter nine examines OSR's history under Casey from January 1981 until OSR's demise in October of that year; it also briefly discusses the continuation of military analysis in CIA through the collapse of the Soviet Union and the end of the Cold War. A major source of information for the chapter is Robert Gates's book, *From the Shadows.*[38] Gates became Casey's chief of staff soon after the new DCI took office, and Casey subsequently appointed him DDI in 1982 and DDCI in 1986. Gates remained the DDCI under William Webster until 1989, and he returned to CIA as the DCI in late 1991 in time to witness the collapse of the Soviet Union.

Casey became DCI with a strong belief that the Agency needed to be strengthened and improved if it was to provide useful intelligence support to President Reagan and his foreign policy advisors. Casey was also the first DCI to become a member of the Cabinet, and he wanted CIA to concentrate on what he saw as the growing Soviet threat to US national security interests, particularly in the Third World. Thus one of Casey's first acts upon taking office was to commission an updated NIE entitled *Soviet Goals and Expectations in the Global Power Arena,* which was issued in July 1981 and was the first done on the topic in several years.[39]

Casey made no immediate changes to NFAC, and he left Clarke in place as its director. However, Clarke did not have a favorable opinion of the new DCI, whom he believed had partisan political views. Casey was a critic of CIA's previous analysis of the Soviet Union,[40] including the strategic forces estimates. Clarke decided to retire in April 1981; he was soon replaced as D/NFAC by John McMahon, who was the deputy director for operations at the time. Huffstutler stayed on as D/OSR and announced another reorganization of OSR soon after McMahon took over. The reorganization was not a major restructuring, but it expanded the global focus of OSR's military analysis by adding Latin America and Africa to its current intelligence and military research responsibilities. In addition, the Strategic Evaluation and Military–Economic Analysis Centers both became divisions with little change in functions.[41]

The new OSR structure did not last long; its demise was to occur only six months later. Soon after McMahon became D/NFAC, he proposed to organize the DDI along regional rather than functional lines to better serve key intelligence consumers, most of whom had a regional focus. By October 1981, with Casey's approval, four former functional offices containing political, economic, military, and societal analysts were integrated into five new regional offices. The bulk of the former OSR managers and analysts were transferred to the new SOVA under Huffstutler. SOVA became the largest and most productive of the regional offices, which included others for the East Asia (OEA), Near East and South Asia (NESA), Europe (EURA), and Africa and Latin America (ALA).[42]

The departure of Clarke in early 1981 and the dissolution of OSR later that year marked the end of a key era of military intelligence analysis in CIA, but OSR's legacy of strong leadership and rigorous analysis lasted for at least another decade. The decline in military analysis in CIA began with the collapse of the Soviet Union in the late 1991 and the subsequent dramatic cutbacks in the number of DI analysts working on the former Soviet Union. The history of this period is another story worth telling, and many former OSR managers and analysts played important roles.

The ***conclusion*** of this study discusses the longer-term impact of the loss of CIA's robust capability to do its own independent analysis of major strategic military threats to US national security interests. Clarke and other former OSR senior managers adamantly believed that despite the end of the Cold War and the rise of international terrorism, foreign military powers and rogue states such as Russia, China, Iran, and North Korea still represented significant threats to US global security interests and that senior policymakers were ill-served by not having CIA provide independent assessments of these threats in competition with the Pentagon.

One of OSR's most important contributions to policymakers was providing them with objective, dispassionate judgments of strategic military threats to vital US foreign policy interests. Former DCIs, such as McCone, Helms, Turner, and Casey, all believed that this was one of CIA's vital roles during the Cold War. The body of this report recounts in some detail how military analysis developed in CIA from its very beginning, including the creation of OSR, until the fall of the Soviet Union.

❖ ❖ ❖

Endnotes

1. Central Intelligence Agency, Directorate of Intelligence, *Directorate of Intelligence: Fifty Years of Informing Policy, Central Intelligence Agency* (CIA), Center for the Study of Intelligence (CSI), 2002, 1–18 and 21–27. Available at www.cia.gov.

2. Details on CIA's early history are partially derived from Knapp, Roberta S., *The Central Intelligence Agency: The First Thirty Years 1947-77*, CIA, History Staff, 1991.

3. NIE 64: *Soviet Bloc Capabilities Through Mid-1953*, 12 November 1952. NIE 90: Soviet Capabilities Through Mid-1955, 18 August 1953.

4. Parkinson, Leonard and Potter, Logan, *The Development of Strategic Intelligence at CIA, 1947-1967*, unpublished draft, 1974. It is available only on request through CSI's History Staff.

5. Steury, Donald, "Strategic Military Analysis in CIA," unpublished draft, 1994. Also available on request from CSI's History Staff.

6. Firth, Noel E. and Noren, James H., *Soviet Defense Spending: A History of CIA Estimates, 1950-1990*, Texas A&M Press, 1998.

7. Smith, Russell Jack, *The Unknown CIA: My Three Decades with the Agency*, Pergamon-Brassey's, 1989, 172-173, 215-216.

8. Turner, Stansfield, *Secrecy and Democracy: The CIA in Transition*, Houghton Mifflin, 1983, 229-251.

9. Gates, Robert M., *From the Shadows: The Ultimate Insider's Story of Five Presidents and How They Won the Cold War*, Simon and Schuster, 1996.

10. Persico, Joseph E., *Casey: From the OSS to the CIA*, Viking, 1990, 209-252.

11. See the bibliography for a complete list of interviews used as sources.

12. Steury, Donald P., editor, *Intentions and Capabilities: Estimates on Soviet Strategic Forces, 1950-1990*, History Staff, CIA, CSI, 1996.

13. Bird, John and Joan, editors, *CIA Analysis of Warsaw Pact Forces: The Importance of Clandestine Reporting*, CIA, CSI, 2014. Available at www.cia.gov.

14. Haines, Gerald K. and Leggett, Robert E., editors, *Watching the Bear: Essays on CIA's Analysis of the Soviet Union*, CIA, CSI, 2002.

15. Haines, Gerald K. and Leggett, Robert E., editors, *CIA's Analysis of the Soviet Union.*

16. Clarke, Bruce C. Jr., "Survey of Military Intelligence Production in the Intelligence Directorate," February 1967.

17. Clarke, Bruce C. Jr., OSR Annual Reports, 1968 to 1973. Available on request from CSI's History Staff. They are located in CIA's archives in Job 79B00039A, Box 2 of 13 Boxes, Folders 9-15, September 1968-1974.

18. OSR Organization and Key Personnel, 7 July 1967 and OSR Personnel Directory, 4 December 1967. OSR organization charts and announcements are located in Job 08-02588R, Box 5 of 6, Folder 26.

19. See NIE 11-8-69, *Soviet Strategic Attack Forces* in Steury, 9 September 1969, 253-61.

20. Smith, *The Unknown CIA*, 205-209 and Helms, Richard, with Hood, William, *A Look over My Shoulder: My Life in the Central Intelligence Agency*, Ballantine Books, 2003, 385-388.

21. Smith, *The Unknown CIA*, 205-209 and Helms, Richard with Hood, William, *My Life in the Central Intelligence Agency*, 385-388.

22. Helms, Richard, Office of the Director, memorandum, "To the People of the Office of Strategic Research," 1 July 1972.

23. Clarke, OSR Organization, 30 June 1972.

24. Firth and Noren, *Soviet Defense Spending*, 46-47.

25. Clarke, OSR Organization, 12 September 1973.

26. Knoche, E. Henry, interviewed by R. Cargill Hall, 24 January 2000.

27. Knoche, OSR Notice, 1 July 1974.

28. Knoche, OSR Organization, 21 September 1973.

29. Lehman, Richard, interviewed by Dick Kovar 29 February 1998.

30. Firth and Noren, *Soviet Defense Spending*, 59-66.

31. The A-Team/B-Team episode is covered in depth by Garthoff, Raymond L., "Soviet Military Capabilities and Intentions," 159-163 in Haines and Leggett, *Watching the Bear.*

32. See NIE 11-3/8-76, *Soviet Forces for Intercontinental Conflict Through the Mid-1980s.*

33. Graybeal, OSR Organization, 8 April 1977.

34. Clarke, Bruce C. Jr., interviewed by Jim Hanrahan, 25 April 2002.

35. See NIE 11-3/8-79, *Soviet Capabilities for Strategic Nuclear Conflict Through the 1980s*.

36. Raymond Garthoff, "Soviet Military Capabilities and Intentions," in Haines and Leggett, *Watching the Bear*, 169-170.

37. The study can be found in Haines and Leggett, *CIA's Analysis of the Soviet Union*, 295-310.

38. Robert Gates, *From the Shadows*.

39. See NIE 11-4-81, *Soviet Goals and Expectations in the Global Power Arena*.

40. Clarke interview, 25 April 2002.

41. Huffstutler, OSR Organization, 9 April 1981.

42. MacMahon, NFAC Reorganization, Agency announcement, 21 September 1981.

❖ ❖ ❖

Chapter One: 1953–61

The Dulles Years and the Growth of CIA's Military Analysis

When President Dwight Eisenhower took office in early 1953, the general consensus among US policymakers was that the primary Soviet military threat to US strategic interests was the presence of large Soviet conventional forces in Eastern Europe and the spread of communism in East Asia, especially in China, North Korea, and Vietnam. At the time, policymakers were not very concerned about the Soviet Union's capability to attack the United States with nuclear weapons. Although the Soviets had tested an atomic device in September 1949, most experts believed that it would take several years for Moscow to build up its nuclear arsenal. Furthermore, the successful US test of a hydrogen weapon in November 1952 increased the confidence of the new Eisenhower administration that the United States had lengthened its strategic nuclear lead over the Soviet Union.

The administration also believed that the United States was well ahead of the Soviet Union in developing advanced bombers capable of intercontinental attack with nuclear weapons. In early 1953, the United States already had a turboprop bomber in its arsenal capable of intercontinental attack, the B-36, as well as the all-jet B-47 medium-range bomber. It had also begun developing the B-52 intercontinental strategic jet bomber, scheduled to enter service in the mid-1950s. As far as US policymakers knew, the Soviets had no equivalent to the B-47 or B-52, and the United States apparently had a three-year lead in bomber aircraft development. An NIE published in August 1953 noted that the Intelligence Community (IC) had no information indicating that series production of a Soviet heavy bomber like the B-52 had begun.[1] On the basis of this assumed strategic advantage, Eisenhower proposed a $5 billion cut to the defense budget to be taken primarily from funding for the US Air Force. Eisenhower was not deterred by the strong negative reaction to the cuts by powerful members of Congress or influential Air Force generals.

Soviet Strategic Surprise

The administration's position would soon change, however. In August 1953, the Soviet Union successfully tested a thermonuclear device. This hydrogen weapon test came as a complete surprise to the IC, which had generally believed that the Soviets were about five years behind in hydrogen bomb development. In fact, the Soviet detonation took place less than a year after the earlier US test. In response to this Soviet strategic surprise and in the wake of the armistice ending the Korean War in July 1953, Eisenhower ordered a major reexamination of US strategic policy and an acceleration of the B-52 bomber program.

The outcome was the Eisenhower administration's new defense policy of "massive retaliation." The policy called for the development of a large nuclear weapons stockpile and sufficient means of delivery to threaten prompt nuclear retaliation against any future communist aggression—conventional, nuclear, or both. The administration also ordered the IC to produce a new assessment of Soviet capabilities to wage general war, including an estimate of the number of Soviet strategic bombers able to carry out a nuclear attack on the United States. In response, CIA produced a special national intelligence estimate (SNIE) in 1954.[2] In the SNIE, Air Force intelligence concluded that a turboprop heavy bomber would likely become the main element in the Soviet strategic air force, and that if series production began in mid-1953, 500 such bombers could be operational by 1957. The SNIE added that if the Soviets undertook a crash program to produce an all-jet bomber like the B-52, 30 could be available by 1957. These estimates were based largely on Western attache sightings of prototype bombers.

The Bomber Gap

In April 1954, US military attaches observed a single Soviet all-jet bomber, the M-4 Bison, rehearsing for the annual May Day air show over Moscow. Air Force intelligence promptly shifted to the view that the Bison would be the mainstay of the Soviet strategic bomber force, projecting that 50 would be produced by 1957 and 250 by 1959. Production of turbo-prop bombers was largely dismissed. These projections appeared in an August 1954 SNIE.[3] Then in early 1955, the Moscow-Fili airframe plant was identified as a Bison production facility, and up to 12 Bison were seen in May Day rehearsals. Air Force intelligence then assessed that the Bison had already been in series production. A new SNIE, issued in June 1955, concluded that the Soviets could have 600 heavy bombers by mid-1958. These included 350 Bison and 250 TU-95 Bear turbo-prop bombers, which were first seen in a Soviet air show in July 1955 and were also assumed to be in series production.[4] Meanwhile, the B-52 bomber was not yet in full production, creating what Congress began referring to as the "bomber gap."

Up to this point, CIA bomber production estimates generally matched those of the Air Force, but this began to change in late 1955. Several individuals played a key role in the development of CIA's capability to do its own analysis of Soviet bomber production and in the subsequent creation of OSR.[5] One of the major players was Dr. Edward Proctor, who had joined CIA in June 1953 from academia with a doctorate in economics. Proctor soon became assistant to the chief of ORR's Industrial Division; then the deputy chief of the Economic Analysis Division, and by 1957, the chief of the Industrial Division, which by then was given the mission of doing checks on military service production estimates. In the wake of the Cuban Missile Crisis, Proctor became the first chief of ORR's new Military-Economic Research Division. He then became deputy in 1966 under R. Jack Smith, and both pushed for the creation of OSR. Proctor succeeded Smith as DDI from May 1971 to June 1976.

Another important player was Howard Stoertz, who had joined CIA in 1950 as an analyst in the Military Division of OCI and moved to the Office of National Estimates (ONE) in 1955. Stoertz became one of ONE's primary specialists in military estimates, and he strongly supported CIA's analysis of Soviet bomber and ICBM production. He also supported the creation of OSR in 1967. Stoertz was to become the first head of the Imagery Analysis Staff (IAS) at NPIC in 1967 and the first NIO for strategic programs in 1973.

A final key role was that of W. Randolph Payne, an aeronautical engineer with previous experience with Lockheed Aircraft Company and a member of ORR's Aircraft Branch in 1954. Payne was responsible for tracking Soviet aircraft production rates; in early 1955, with the assistance of the US aircraft industry, he developed a new methodology for estimating Soviet bomber production. Payne also set up a training course on the methodology for Aircraft Branch analysts beginning in July 1955. The branch then began to revise its Bison and Bear production estimates based on more detailed intelligence information that it began to acquire. Payne became a deputy division chief when OSR was created in 1967.

Community Disagreements

When a new NIE on Soviet capabilities to attack the United States was completed in March 1956, ORR disagreed with Air Force's future production rates of heavy bombers, particularly for Bear heavy bombers.[6] ONE wanted to use a lower force projection, but DCI Allen Dulles objected to CIA challenging the higher Air Force production estimates. Nevertheless, the Army, Navy, and State Department all took a footnote stating that the number of heavy bombers could be far fewer than the Air Force estimates. When Dulles briefed a Senate Armed Services subcommittee on Soviet bomber production in April 1956, he acknowledged that the members of the Intelligence Community disagreed on Bear production in the March NIE. He was asked to return with an agreed Community bomber estimate.

Howard Stoertz, who had helped prepare the NIE, tried to resolve the differences, but he was unable to do so. The differences intensified after Western attaches obtained serial numbers of new Bison and Bear during rehearsals for the 1956 May Day celebrations. The Air Force and CIA's Air Branch had different interpretations of the data, and they also disagreed on the number of aircraft plants that were building heavy bombers and the production rates at each plant. In the end, they compromised by agreeing to lower current production estimates for both Bison and Bear bombers while retaining high future force projections in a new NIE completed in August 1956. The new numbers agreed to by the Community were 40 Bison and 40 Bear bombers produced by mid-1956 and a projected total of 500 Bison and 300 Bear produced by mid-1960.[7]

The next estimate to address the bomber issue was NIE 11-4-57, *Main Trends in Soviet Capabilities and Policies: 1957-1962*, completed in November 1957.[8] By this time, Payne and the Aircraft Branch had completed a detailed study of Soviet bomber production using additional serial numbers, newly available imagery from the first series of U-2 flights beginning in mid-1956, and a careful examination of production rates, particularly at the Moscow-Fili airframe facility. For example, CIA assessed that the Bison production rate was three to four aircraft per month at the Fili facility, while the Air Force still believed it was 15 per month. The CIA draft was provided to Stoertz, who tried to resolve the differences between the lower CIA and higher Air Force production bomber production estimates but again failed to do so.

When Dulles became aware of the continued differences, he asked his deputy DCI (DDCI), Air Force Gen. Charles Cabell, to see whether he could get CIA and Air Force to agree on compromise numbers. Cabell contacted Proctor, who was then chief of ORR's Industrial Division, and asked him to attend a meeting with Air Force intelligence officers to try to reach a compromise. Proctor took along Randy Payne from the Aircraft Branch. After hearing the Air Force assessments, both individuals refused to agree to the higher Air Force Bison and Bear production rates. Cabell never pressured CIA to back off; the two sides agreed to disagree.

As a result, the 1957 NIE was different than the previous estimates on the subject, which used only Air Force or compromise bomber production numbers and projections. The NIE avoided open disagreement in the main text by including both CIA and Air Force production numbers without departmental attribution and by presenting a range of the two estimates in an accompanying table. The lower numbers represented CIA's estimate and the higher numbers Air Force's estimate. The current mid-1957 force level was a range of 90–50 Bison and Bear heavy bombers, and the projected mid-1960 force level was a range of 400–600 heavy bombers. The NIE noted that the future force projection was lower than in previous estimates. The Joint Chiefs of Staff (JCS), the Army, and the Navy all took a footnote disagreeing with the higher numbers, and the Air Force disagreed with the lower numbers.

Proctor regarded the 1957 estimate as a major breakthrough for ORR. For the first time, Dulles had allowed the NIE to include ORR's estimates of the number of Soviet heavy bombers in production—thus ORR's assessment would reach a wider national policy audience. Furthermore, despite the nonattribution, the CIA production numbers represented a direct challenge to the Air Force estimates. The author of this study does not know why Dulles agreed to support the independent CIA assessment. Several factors may have been in play. President Eisenhower was known to disagree with the high Air Force bomber projections, causing him considerable political problems with Congress. Also, the State Department had disagreed with the high Air Force Soviet bomber numbers in the 1956 NIE, and Secretary of State John Foster Dulles may have influenced his brother to use a range of estimates in the 1957 NIE. Finally, Sherman Kent and Stoertz were both strong advocates of independent CIA analysis on key military issues and may have had some influence on the DCI.

The bomber gap began to fade as an issue in late 1957 as information became available that Bison production rates at Moscow-Fili were falling. A 1958 SNIE dramatically lowered the future Soviet bomber force projection to only 100–200 heavy bombers by mid-1960, adding that the Soviets would be likely to rely on ICBMs for intercontinental delivery of nuclear weapons by mid-1963.[9] The bomber gap issue was not fully resolved until the advent of US satellite imagery in the early 1960s provided much more accurate intelligence on Soviet strategic force levels. In fact, the Soviets stopped production of the Bison in 1963, with only about 90 bomber and tanker versions ever produced. Instead, the Bear was to become the mainstay of the Soviet heavy bomber force. It remains in service to this day, with over 500 bomber, tanker, and reconnaissance versions having been produced.

The Missile Gap

While the bomber gap issue began to fade, the so-called "missile-gap" issue gained prominence as a new intelligence and political controversy. Concern that US intelligence had greatly underestimated the pace of Soviet missile development was triggered by two events in late 1957: the first Soviet intercontinental ballistic missile (ICBM) tests on 26 August and 7 September 1957 and the first launches of the Sputnik earth-orbiting satellites on 4 October 1957 and 3 November 1957. The reaction in Congress and by the Eisenhower administration was immediate. Various congressional inquiries were launched to assess the status of Soviet and US ICBM programs, and the White House appointed Dr. James R. Killian, the president of MIT, to the new post of special assistant to the president for science and technology to oversee the US strategic missile program.

Once again, Ed Proctor and ORR, as well as OSI, would play a role in CIA's response to the evolving missile-gap issue, and once again, CIA's analysis of the Soviet ICBM program would clash with the Air Force's intelligence analysis. A major difference compared with the bomber gap issue, however, was that much less information was available on the status of the Soviet missile programs than on the bomber programs. Nevertheless, CIA employed its collection resources and analytic expertise far more effectively than the Air Force. By the time the missile-gap issue was resolved through analysis of satellite imagery in the early 1960s, CIA had become preeminent in the IC on the subject of Soviet ICBMs.[10]

CIA had produced three NIEs on Soviet ICBM development from October 1954 to March 1957, all with significant contributions from ORR and OSI. The first and most comprehensive was NIE 11-6-54, *Soviet Capabilities and Probable Programs in the Guided Missile Field.*[11] This estimate, which was produced in response to a request from the administration, assessed all Soviet guided-missile programs. The program of greatest concern was the ICBM program, about which very little was known. ONE established an ad hoc committee to achieve coordination among the various intelligence agencies on the major contributions to the estimate. It was chaired by Proctor, who was then assistant chief of the Industrial Division in ORR.

From the very start of the estimative process, rivalry arose between ORR and OSI over how the NIE should be done. H. Marshall Chadwell, head of OSI at the time, had established the first component in CIA for research and development on Soviet guided missiles in 1953. OSI wanted an NIE that focused on the scientific and technical aspects of the missile program, relying heavily on data from returning German missile specialists and scant communications intelligence (COMINT) intercepts on missile development programs. Edward Allen, the chief of the Economic Research Area (ERA) in ORR, wanted to go further and analyze the resources available for the missile programs and the cost of the effort to the Soviet economy. The ORR approach prevailed with ONE; nevertheless, OSI contributed considerable resources and expertise to the CIA contribution on the technical aspects of Soviet missiles.

The approach that Allen used for the CIA contribution to the NIE was to take the military services' assessments of the various Soviet missile programs and, with support from OSI, direct ERA to evaluate the financial cost of the programs and the industrial capacity to support them. Most of ERA was involved in the analysis, particularly for estimates of industrial capacity, but the chief analytic effort centered in the Aircraft Branch and the Military Economics Branch. The Aircraft Branch estimated the production capacity for missiles, and the Military Economics Branch estimated the cost of the missile programs and their impact on the Soviet economy. The results of this building-block approach to estimating the cost of various Soviet guided-missile systems was a key CIA contribution to NIE 11-6-54, and only the Military Economics Branch could do the costing effort. Allen had personally selected the first chief of the branch, John Godaire, to lead the effort; Godaire would continue to play a major role in developing CIA's military costing capabilities for the next two decades.[12]

ONE accepted this costing methodology, which was used in the next two guided-missile estimates to check on the service estimates of military hardware. To improve CIA analytic support to the estimative process, DDI Robert Amory approved the expansion of OSI's Guided Missile Branch to a full division in March 1955. Soon after, Allen formed a Guided Missile Task Force under Proctor to coordinate and produce all economic intelligence on Soviet guided missiles within ORR. The staff included Randy Payne and two analysts from Industrial Division, Roland Inlow and Clarence W. Baier, both of whom would go on to hold senior positions in the future OSR. Finally, in early 1957, Proctor became chief of ORR's Industrial Division and created a new Guided Missile Branch under Inlow.

The major judgment of the 1954 NIE was that conclusive evidence showed a large and active Soviet research and development program for guided missiles, but very little any information was available on individual missiles under development or in production, particularly for ICBMs. Nevertheless, the NIE concluded that a Soviet ICBM could be deployed as early as 1960 but more likely by 1963. An updated NIE was issued in December 1955 using the same methodology. It moved the likely ICBM deployment date up to 1960–61 and added that the Soviets could place a satellite in earth-orbit by 1958.[13] The next NIE in the series, issued in March 1957, did not change any of the main judgments but estimated that the Soviets might eventually produce 1,000 ICBMs by 1965 and already had the capability to orbit a satellite.[14]

The production of these three NIEs on Soviet guided missiles led to several important results before the surprise ICBM and satellite launches in late 1957. First, Dulles made intelligence collection on Soviet guided missiles the highest priority for the entire IC in late 1955. As a result, the U-2 program was accelerated, and the first photographic missions were flown over the Soviet Union in June and July 1956. In addition, radar stations were established along the southern perimeter of the Soviet Union to monitor ICBM testing activity. Next, with the support of Secretary of Defense Charles Wilson, the DCI established a Guided Missile Intelligence Committee in early 1956 to oversee Intelligence Community efforts on the issue. At the same time, DoD agreed that the subject of guided missiles was a national intelligence responsibility, not a departmental one.

In the wake of the Soviet ICBM tests and Sputnik launches in late 1957, several new estimates were commissioned to address the status of the Soviet ICBM program and set a projected date by which the Soviets would be able to deploy an operational ICBM force. The first in the series, SNIE 11-10-57, *The Soviet ICBM Program*, can be considered the beginning of the missile-gap controversy.[15] By this time, U-2 imagery of the Tyuratam ICBM missile test facility had been obtained, and the missile tested had been identified as the SS-6 ICBM. Nevertheless, no ICBM production facility had yet been identified, nor had any deployed operational ICBM launch facility. As a result, the SNIE arbitrarily postulated a "first operational capability" as deployment of ten missiles, and a "substantial operational capability" as 500 deployed missiles. Based on ORR analysis of production capabilities, it projected a force of ten ICBMs by mid-1959, 100 by mid-1960, and 500 by mid-1962. US ICBM force deployment projections were several years behind, raising intense political concern in Congress. The next estimate in the series, NIE 11-5-58, added no new intelligence insights and made no major changes to the future force projections.

This soon changed, however, beginning with the next guided missile estimates completed in late 1959 and early 1960. By that time, Soviet Premier Nikita Khrushchev had announced that the Soviet Union had the capability to mass-produce ICBMs and attack aggressors anywhere in the world. To complete the estimates, Kent requested that Proctor be detailed full time to the ONE staff. The first estimate, NIE 11-5-59, was issued in November 1959 and was essentially a reference aid that made no new projections of ICBM force levels.[16] The next estimate, NIE 11-8-59, was not issued until early 1960 because of major disagreements with the Air Force over projected future ICBM force levels.[17] The initial ICBM force of ten missiles was projected to be operational by early 1960 and a force of 35 missiles with four launchers by mid-1960. Beyond 1960, a range of missile projections were provided: 140–200 by mid-1961, 250–350 by mid-1962, and 350–450 by mid-1963. The Air Force projected that the Soviets would have a force of 385 missiles by mid-1962 and 640 by mid-1963, adding in a footnote that the Soviets were aiming for decisive military superiority over the United States rather than only a deterrence or a preemptive attack capability.

Dulles used NIE 11-8-59 as the basis for his key testimony to a joint Senate committee hearing on 29 January 1960 chaired by then Senator Lyndon Johnson. He took his deputy, General Cabell; Director of OSI Scoville; Proctor from ORR; and Stoertz from ONE. The extremely acrimonious hearing was the roughest congressional missile-gap proceeding on record, and it would have political repercussions in the 1960 presidential election. The harsh questioning underscored the lack of firm evidence of Soviet force levels before the deployment of US reconnaissance satellites in the early 1960s, which ended the so-called "dark era" of strategic analysis.

Dulles angrily returned to CIA after the hearing and immediately intensified CIA collection and analytic efforts against Soviet ICBMs. Inlow was asked to brief Dulles on analytic issues pertaining to ICBM deployment. In defense of the NIE, Inlow stated that it was controversial because of disagreements in the IC over Soviet motivations to build a large strategic missile force to confront the United States. The alternative reasons were that Moscow wanted dominant military superiority, a high level of deterrence, a modest first-strike capability, or some combination of the three. Inlow added that despite the general consensus that the Soviets were determined to build a large strategic missile force, not a single ICBM launch site had been detected. To ensure that CIA was not missing something, DDI Amory suggested the formation of an ad hoc Guided Missile Task Force, and Dulles promptly agreed. With Proctor as chief and Inlow as his deputy, it included 30 analysts from both ORR and OSI.

The collection effort against the Soviet Union took a major hit with the 1 May 1960 shootdown of the U-2 flown by Francis Gary Powers, who was conducting a reconnaissance mission over the Soviet Union. Following the shootdown, the overflights were ended. The estimate produced in the wake of the incident, NIE 11-8-60, *Soviet Capabilities for Long-Range Attack Through Mid-1965*, issued in August 1960, caused an unprecedented level of acrimony within the IC on the issue of Soviet ICBM deployment.[18] Although evidence of continued ICBM testing existed, none indicated deployment. One explanation was that vast areas of the Soviet Union had not been covered by the U-2 program. The absence of any meaningful intelligence about a full-scale ICBM production program was harder to explain away, and no production facilities had been confirmed.

Unable to resolve significant differences regarding ICBM force levels, the NIE postulated three potential Soviet missile programs. Program "A," which estimated a force of 400 ICBMs by mid-1963 and representing a strategic deterrent capability, was the DCI's pick. The Air Force favored Program "B," which estimated a Soviet ICBM force of 700 by mid-1963, representing a decisive Soviet strategic superiority. The Army and Navy favored Program "C," which projected a force of only 200 ICBMs by mid-1963. The State Department favored a force within the "A-B" range. Most IC agencies agreed that then current deployed force contained only a few ICBMs. In all, the estimate had 36 dissenting footnotes. While most IC organizations assessed that the Soviets were building a strategic missile force primarily to deter a US attack, the Air Force continued to dissent, judging that the Soviets sought to attain military superiority over the United States and a preemptive first-strike capability.

The End of the Controversy

Shortly after the dissemination of this contentious estimate, a series of closely spaced collection breakthroughs marked the beginning of the end of the missile-gap controversy. The most significant was the successful launch on 18 August 1960 of the first photographic collection mission by a US reconnaissance satellite, the KH-4. This covert CIA program, code-named CORONA, had been approved by President Eisenhower in February 1958. The resolution of the KH-4 cameras was less than that of the U-2's cameras, but the area of coverage was much greater, and each KH-4 mission was able to collect more usable photography of the Soviet Union than all 24 previous U-2 missions combined.

The photography from each KH-4 mission was sent to CIA's Photographic Intelligence Center (PIC), created in August 1958 and headed by Arthur Lundahl. The PIC was formerly the Photo-Intelligence Division of ORR, also under Lundahl, and it had previously exploited U-2 photography. In preparation for the CORONA missions, a joint ORR-OSI team was assigned in June 1959 to help the PIC determine the highest-priority collection targets and how to best process the anticipated high volume of data. The team included Bill Baier from ORR and Sidney Graybeal from OSI. The two leaders recommended the creation of an all-source database capable of computer storage and prepared a list of some 1,500 individual missile targets, including potential production facilities and launch sites. As a result, the PIC was ready to handle the data from the first and successive CORONA missions.

The next KH-4 mission, which took place in December 1960, provided the first photographic coverage of a deployed Soviet SS-6 ICBM missile site at Plesetsk. It led to the first all-source intelligence report using CORONA photography. Done by Proctor's Guided Missile Task Force, the report would become a standard for the new era of extensive use of satellite imagery for military analysis. As the volume of KH-4 data increased, more missile-related facilities were discovered, and in January 1961, the National Photographic Interpretation Center (NPIC) was created under Lundahl in the Directorate of Intelligence (DI) to provide photographic support to the entire IC. Soon after, a second ICBM launch complex was confirmed on photography at Yur'ya, but no other missiles sites were discovered, raising serious doubts that the SS-6 had been widely deployed.

The second intelligence breakthrough on the Soviet missile program occurred in February and March 1961, when data on ICBM launches confirmed that a new missile, later designated the SS-7, had entered the test-range phase. Then in April, data on another test launch confirmed the arrival of another new ICBM, the SS-8. Although not immediately apparent, the IC eventually confirmed that the SS-6 program had been abandoned in favor of two second-generation ICBMs then under development. The SS-6 was large and difficult to handle because its liquid fuel was hard to store. The smaller SS-7 and SS-8 ICBMs used solid fuel and could be deployed in silos.

A Hoax

The third breakthrough involved Soviet Col. Oleg Penkovsky, a military intelligence officer who made contact with CIA and British intelligence in August 1960. During the next two years, Penkovsky provided a vast store of intelligence on Soviet strategic thinking and Moscow's key missile programs. He described the missile gap as a "hoax," saying that Khrushchev wanted to foster the impression of a massive Soviet missile program at a time when such a program was virtually nonexistent.

In the next estimate on the Soviet ICBM program, NIE 11-8-61, issued in June 1961, the IC substantially reduced its projections of Soviet ICBM force levels, thereby reducing the perceived missile gap.

Nevertheless, the range of projections remained wide, and only the Air Force held out for a substantially larger future force beyond the accepted ranges. A follow-up estimate, NIE 11-8/1-61, issued in September 1961, put the concept of a missile gap to rest in its opening sentence: "New information, providing a much firmer base for estimates on Soviet long-range missiles, has caused a sharp downward revision in our estimate of present Soviet ICBM strength."[19] Based on CORONA photography, the new estimate concluded that only 10–25 missile launchers were currently deployed, and that such a force level would not increase markedly in the ensuing months.

The main result of the bomber- and missile-gap controversies from CIA's perspective is that by the beginning of the 1960s, military analysis in the DDI was firmly established. The military intelligence services no longer played a dominant role in producing national intelligence estimates on military-related issues. DCI Dulles and ONE Chairman Sherman Kent had come to accept that CIA could make a major contribution to the estimative process through its expertise on Soviet defense spending and the costing of major weapons systems and other military expenditures. During the next decade, CIA would become increasingly responsible for providing military intelligence support to US policymakers, not only through the estimative process but also in direct support of strategic policy debates and decisionmaking. This was clearly the case in the first major strategic challenge to confront the new Kennedy administration, the Cuban Missile Crisis.

❖ ❖ ❖

Endnotes

1. CIA, NIE 90, *Soviet Bloc Capabilities Through Mid-1955*, 18 August 1953. A listing of declassified national intelligence estimates on the Soviet Union to 1984 can be found in CIA, CSI, *Declassified National Intelligence Estimates on the Soviet Union and International Communism, 1946-1984*.

2. CIA, SNIE 11-54, *Likelihood of a General War Through 1957*, 15 February 1954.

3. CIA,. SNIE 11-7-54, *Soviet Gross Capabilities for Attacks on the U.S. and Key Overseas Installations Through 1 July 1957*, 17 August 1954.

4. CIA. NIE 11-7-54, *Soviet Gross Capabilities for Attacks on the U.S. and Key Overseas Installations and Forces*, 23 June 1955.

5. Details on how the CIA got heavily involved in the "bomber-gap" controversy and the key individuals who played a major role in CIA's analysis of the issue are derived primarily from Parkinson and Potter, *The Development of Strategic Intelligence at CIA*, 65-108. In addition, Steury, *Intentions and Capabilities: Estimates of Soviet Strategic Forces, 1950-1990*, contains a series of unclassified versions of CIA estimates relating to the issue. Finally, see Garthoff, Raymond L., "Estimating Soviet Military Capabilities and Intentions," in Haines and Leggett, *Watching the Bear*, 135-186, for a detailed analysis of CIA's Soviet strategic estimates during the Cold War era.

6. CIA. NIE-56, *Soviet Gross Capabilities for Attack on the U.S. and Key Overseas Installations Through Mid-1959*, 6 March 1956.

7. CIA. NIE 11-4-56, *Soviet Capabilities and Probable Courses of Action Through 1961*, 2 August 1956.

8. CIA. NIE 11-4-57, *Main Trends in Soviet Capabilities and Policies*, 12 November 1957.

9. CIA. NIE 11-7-58, *Strength and Capabilities of the Soviet Long-Range Bomber Force*, 5 June 1958.

10. Details on how CIA responded to the "missile-gap" controversy are derived primarily from Parkinson and Potter, *The Development of Strategic Research in CIA*, 109-235. Relevant CIA estimates can be found in Steury, *Intentions and Capabilities*, 55-138. The issue is also covered in some detail in Garthoff, "Estimating Soviet Intentions and Capabilities," 140-147.

11. CIA, NIE-11-6-54, *Soviet Capabilities and Probable Programs in the Guided Missile Field*, 5 October 1954.

12. Firth and Noren, *Soviet Defense Spending*, 30-33.

13. NIE 11-12-55, *Soviet Guided Missile Capabilities and Probable Programs*, 20 December 1955.

14. CIA. NIE 11-12-55, *Soviet Guided Missile Capabilities and Probable Programs*, 20 December 1955 and NIE 11-5-57, *Soviet Capabilities and Probable Programs in the Guided Missile Field*, 12 March 1957.

15. CIA. SNIE 11-10-57, *The Soviet ICBM Program*, 10 December 1957.

16. CIA. NIE 11-5-59, *Soviet Capabilities in Guided Missiles and Space Vehicles*, 3 November 1959.

17. CIA. NIE 11-8-59, *Soviet Capabilities for Strategic Attack Through Mid-1964*, 9 February 1960.

18. CIA. NIE 11-8-60, *Soviet Capabilities for Long-Range Attack Through Mid-1965*, 1 August 1960.

19. CIA. NIE 11-8-61, *Soviet Capabilities for Long-Range Attack*, 7 June 1961 and NIE 11-8/1-61, *Strength and Deployment of Soviet Long-Range Ballistic Missile Forces*, 21 September 1961.

❖ ❖ ❖

Chapter Two: 1961–67

The McCone Years and Increased Support to Policymakers on Strategic Military Issues

The bomber- and missile-gap issues were important watersheds for military analysis at CIA under DCI Dulles, but the Cuban Missile Crisis was an even greater test of CIA's analytic capabilities. Most significant, it helped restore President John F. Kennedy's confidence in CIA. When McCone took over as DCI in late 1961, he was already sympathetic to Secretary of Defense Robert McNamara's systems-analysis approach to assessing foreign military threats, which required detailed intelligence on enemy military programs. McCone decided that CIA needed to reach its own conclusions in the fragmented field of strategic military intelligence. As a result, he approved several measures to enhance CIA's capability to do independent military analysis and provide more direct and frequent intelligence support to military planners at DoD and to members of the NSC.

Soon after McCone's arrival, DDI Robert Amory took the first of several major steps to consolidate and improve CIA's capability to do more comprehensive and better integrated military analysis. In January 1962, he accepted a proposal by the chief of the Office of Scientific Intelligence (OSI), Herbert "Pete" Scoville, to reorganize the existing branches in OSI into offensive and defensive missile divisions. This would help meet the Pentagon's need for greater emphasis on the weapons-system and military-mission approaches to defense program analysis. To head the Offensive Missile Division, Scoville selected

Graybeal, who was to play an important role in providing intelligence during the Cuban Missile Crisis.

Soon after, Ray Cline replaced Amory as DDI. In April 1962 Cline approved a proposal to create a new Military-Economic Division in the Office of Research and Reports (ORR). Proctor had formulated the idea in late 1961 while he headed the Guided Missile Task Force. Proctor reasoned that the new emphasis on systems analysis required a military division that would bring together military analysts in the Industrial Division and in the task force to expand the scope of strategic military research in CIA. When Cline approved the proposal, he added the word "economic" to the title, perhaps to soften the services' opposition to the creation of a military research division in CIA. The new division was established in May 1962 with Proctor as chief and Inlow as his deputy. It had a Plans and Support Staff and over 50 personnel divided among six branches. Four were weapons systems branches (aircraft, naval, guided-missile production, and guided-missile deployment); the other branches were military programming and military expenditures.

Another DI reorganization took place in the summer of 1962, led by R. Jack Smith. Cline had selected Smith in April 1962 to take over OCI from Huntington Sheldon. Cline and Smith were close friends with similar academic and intelligence backgrounds. They had worked together for the OSS during World War II after Cline offered Smith a job there; Smith returned the favor by getting Cline a job at CIA in 1949. The two men also subsequently worked together on the ONE staff. Smith strongly believed that OCI should do a better job of producing current intelligence on military issues for senior policymakers. Cline agreed, and Smith undertook a major expansion of OCI by strengthening its small Military Division.[1] Smith issued a new charter for the division in August 1962, stating that it must be competent to determine what information is significant and newsworthy in the realm of military affairs and related scientific and economic areas. He added that the division should consider the views of other offices having primary competence in these fields (i.e. ORR and OSI) but that the Military Division should have final say on the newsworthiness of an item.

Smith added that the enlarged division should be organized along mission and functional lines rather than by individual military services. The two main components were a Theater Branch and a Strategic Branch. The Theater Branch covered Soviet Bloc ground forces; sea forces, except for long-range missile submarines; tactical air forces; and air defense. Strategic Branch covered long-range attack forces, space developments, and advanced weapons programs. Smith concluded that the division must obtain the competence necessary to do its work by intensive analysis of Soviet military doctrine, close liaison with related intelligence components, a sustained relationship with government and private research and development organizations, and frequent visits to US military installations.

In September 1962, Smith asked Bruce Clarke, who was then chief of Research Division in the DI's Office of Basic Intelligence (OBI), to lead OCI's Military Division. Clarke had joined CIA in 1953 after serving as an intelligence officer in the US Navy. He was a graduate of both Syracuse University and the Sorbonne, and his father had been a distinguished Army general in World War II. Clarke started out in the Basic Intelligence Division of ORR, working on military intelligence. When the division became an office in 1955, Clarke became the special assistant to the director. In 1959, he joined the ONE staff, where he worked with Smith in drafting NIEs. Clarke returned to OBI in 1961 to head the newly created Research Division. When that unit was transferred to OCI in early 1982, Smith offered Clarke the opportunity to become the head of the Military Division, and Clarke readily accepted. Smith explained to Clarke that Clarke had Cline's approval to fill out the new division by transferring personnel from the Research Division. For a time, Clarke was concurrently chief of both divisions; he began working full time in the Military Division in mid-September, just before the outbreak of the Cuban Missile Crisis.[2]

The Cuban Missile Crisis

As a result of the reorganizations in OSI, ORR, and OCI, Cline and the DI were ready and able to provide crucial intelligence support to McCone and the Kennedy administration during the onset of the Cuban

Missile Crisis in late 1962. Several individuals in all three offices were to play key roles in the crisis, as were others in the DI who would subsequently hold senior management positions in CIA. These included Proctor, who was given an Intelligence Letter of Merit as head of OCI's Military-Economic Division; Graybeal, who, as head of OSI's Offensive Missile Division briefed President Kennedy on the initial discovery of Soviet SS-4 MRBMs and SS-5 IRBMs in Cuba; and Clarke, who as head of the newly created Military Division in OCI set up a "situation room" to provide current intelligence support to policymakers during the crisis. In addition, Arthur Lundahl, director of NPIC, provided regular updates to senior policymakers using photos from the latest overhead reconnaissance missions.[3]

The Cuban Missile Crisis provided a unique opportunity for Clarke to demonstrate that the Military Division could work effectively with other DI components to provide integrated military intelligence support to policymakers. As concern began to mount in mid-1962 over the possibility of Soviet missile shipments to Cuba, Clarke divided the division into two groups, one to concentrate on developments in the Soviet Union and the other to staff the situation room, which Clarke created in mid-September. He picked his deputy, John Hicks, to run the situation room, which was staffed with analysts from both Military Division and from various branches in ORR, especially the Transportation Branch, which was closely monitoring all Soviet military shipments to Cuba.

On 15 October 1962, imagery analysts definitively identified offensive missile sites in Cuba on U-2 photography, and the situation room began issuing daily all-source intelligence reports. The reports were based primarily on findings from various CIA components—including the ORR, OSI, and OCI—as well as NPIC. CIA analysts concentrated on developments in and around Cuba as well as on military activities in the Soviet Union. As the crisis mounted, the reports helped assure policymakers that, despite escalating tensions with Moscow, no significant military mobilization was taking place in the Soviet Union.

Expanded Mandate

Cline must have been very pleased with OCI's performance during the crisis, because once it receded, he increasingly turned to Smith on problems concerning strategic weapon systems that went beyond the competence of any one DDI component. Smith, in turn, called on Clarke to coordinate the effort and pull the results together. One special application of this approach was to make Military Division responsible for the preliminary assessment of each new photographic satellite mission. Meanwhile, Clarke fully implemented Smith's August directive to adopt a weapons-system approach by establishing Strategic Forces and Theater Forces Branches and assisting in the merger of the former OBI division into OCI. Clarke also established a Scientific and Technical Branch, headed by Hicks, to overcome a problem of several years' standing: the lack of current reporting on the military significance of OSI's intelligence findings.

Tension between military analysts in OCI (and later OSR) on the one hand and scientific analysts in OSI on the other over current intelligence reporting was a persistent problem, and the issue was never fully resolved. The two organizations had different intelligence objectives, methods of operation, and reporting styles. Military Division analysts sought to report on at least the general significance of scientific and technical intelligence pertaining to military capabilities. OSI analysts generally were reluctant to report anything beyond specific details, particularly until all the data were obtained and analyzed. They were concerned that a lay consumer would misinterpret the significance of current intelligence reports written in general terms. Problems with OSI coordination notwithstanding, both Smith and Clarke were convinced that OCI had the CIA charter and responsibility to report scientific and technical developments of interest to consumers on a timely basis.

With Smith's support, Clarke took an aggressive approach to current intelligence production. Clarke decided to use the Current Intelligence Weekly Review (CIWR) as the primary vehicle for expressing CIA's view on military intelligence matters. Unlike the Current Intelligence Bulletin (CIB), which was coordinated with the rest of the Intelligence

Community, the CIWR was a departmental product, not a national intelligence publication. Military Division took the lead in determining what intelligence was suitable for publication; although the division considered the views of other CIA components, it did not allow other components to veto any given material. Meanwhile, Military Division continued to produce occasional items for the CIB as well as the *President's Daily Brief* (PDB), which CIA produced for the president and his closest advisers. This publication started out as the *President's Intelligence Checklist* in June 1961 for President Kennedy as a concise publication with material too sensitive for the CIB. After President Johnson assumed office on 22 November 1963, OCI turned the *Checklist* into the PDB in 1964.

Creation of the DS&T

One of DCI McCone's most significant organizational changes in CIA in the wake of the Cuban Missile Crisis was the creation of the new Directorate of Science and Technology (DS&T) under Albert "Bud" Wheelon in August 1963. McCone had long wanted to consolidate and improve CIA's scientific and technical capabilities, which were divided primarily between the DI and the clandestine service. In early 1962, he selected Herbert Scoville, then head of OSI, to create a proposed new directorate of research. Scoville failed at the task of creating a robust new organization, primarily because of strong opposition from the DDI, which contained OCI and NPIC, and the clandestine services, which ran CIA's overhead reconnaissance and technical tradecraft programs. Scoville resigned in June 1963, and McCone asked Wheelon to replace him. Wheelon agreed on the condition that he be allowed to create a robust line organization.

Wheelon, who had a PhD in physics from MIT and a powerful personality, was up to the task. During the next two years as DDS&T under McCone, Wheelon put together the most powerful development and engineering organization in the Intelligence Community. He began by integrating OSI from the DDI and the Office of Computer Services from the Directorate of Support into the new directorate. By early 1964, the DS&T had six offices: Scientific Intelligence, Computer

Services, electronic intelligence (ELINT), Research and Development, Special Activities, and the Foreign Missile and Space Analysis Center (FMSAC). The only two scientific and technical components in CIA not included in the DS&T were the Technical Services Division, which was part of the clandestine services; and NPIC, which came under the DI.

McCone had created FMSAC in November 1963 despite strong opposition from the Pentagon, particularly the Air Force, which saw it as duplicating DoD missile and space intelligence efforts. McCone selected Carl Duckett, a missile expert at the Army's Redstone Arsenal, to head the new center. Its mission was to process and analyze all missile and space intelligence, including technical details of Soviet, Chinese, and other foreign space and missile systems.

Conflict soon developed between the DI and the DS&T on intelligence reporting responsibilities. The DCI's office had to intervene to resolve the dispute. The DI agreed that Wheelon's directorate would produce intelligence on scientific and technical subjects for select policymakers and for contributions to national intelligence estimates, as well as represent the DCI on IC scientific committees. The DI retained the overall responsibility for producing and disseminating finished intelligence on scientific issues outside CIA after coordination with OSI, and the DI would represent the Agency's analytic position for NIEs and other national intelligence products.

Controversial National Intelligence Estimates (NIEs)

Meanwhile, the DDI's support to the estimative process began to evolve under DCI McCone. In April 1961, the RAND Corporation completed a study requested by DDI Amory to examine how to improve estimates of Soviet military forces. The report, titled "Project Lamp," called for the adoption of a systems analysis approach to Soviet military estimates, including a military mission format (i.e., strategic offensive, strategic defense, and general-purpose or theater forces), a five-year projection of force levels with a consideration of likely alternatives, and deeper analysis of Soviet military expenditures. It also called for greater consideration of Soviet military doctrine and strategy. ONE promptly began to consider weapon systems rather than force levels and gave greater emphasis to Soviet military research and development, Soviet strategic thinking, and Soviet military planning. A primary concern was the need for improved costing methodologies to support future force projections.[4]

Unlike Dulles, McCone took a strong personal interest in all the NIEs about the Soviet Union, probably because he was well aware of their potential impact on US defense policy. He participated in the drafting and adjudication of these estimates more than most DCIs before or since, with the possible exception of DCI Turner. In addition, in response to the Lamp study recommendation for alternative force levels, the estimates began to include alternative Soviet military force structures rather than a range of force projections. Proctor's new Military-Economic Division played a major role in supporting the new estimative process. In 1962, it made an important contribution to NIE 11-8-62, which updated the IC's projections of Soviet strategic attack capabilities.[5] Compared to its predecessor estimate, NIE 11-8/1-61,[6] the estimate made much greater use of satellite photography to project current and future Soviet strategic force levels with greater accuracy; in addition, it cited material from Soviet defector Oleg Penkovsky to discuss Soviet military strategy. The division also made a major contribution to two new estimates added to the military series: NIE 11-3-62 on Soviet Bloc air and missile defense capabilities and NIE 11-14-62 on Soviet theater forces. These estimates, issued in late 1962, rounded out the group of estimates keyed to the Pentagon's interest in examining Soviet forces according to their missions.

The main topics of all three of these estimates were controversial, and all caused further disputes between CIA and the military intelligence agencies, including the new Defense Intelligence Agency (DIA) established by McNamara in October 1961. Much to McCone's dismay, the Air Force disagreed with the basic judgment of NIE 11-8-62, which stated that the Soviets were not embarking on a crash program to build ICBMs. In the NIE most IC organizations judged that during the ensuing five years, Soviet strategic forces would grow at a slower rate than those of the United States. The Air Force took a footnote, arguing that the Soviets would build twice as many ICBMs by 1967 as projected in the estimate. McCone tried to get Air Force to change its position right up until he resigned as DCI in April 1965, but to no avail. Air Force continued to dissent, taking footnotes in subsequent Soviet strategic estimates in the mid-1960s that projected higher Soviet ICBM force levels through the end of the decade. Basically, Air Force continued to assess that Moscow intended to achieve strategic nuclear superiority over the United States.[7]

The ABM Controversy

CIA disagreements with Air Force also arose over the issue of whether the Soviets intended to build a robust anti-ballistic missile (ABM) system. The first Soviet air defense site built for an ABM system had been identified near Leningrad in 1961; the Community took a cautious approach in NIE 11-3-62 regarding whether the system was an ABM system or one intended to defend against strategic bomber attacks. Subsequent satellite imagery indicated that the Soviets had abandoned the Leningrad site and were building new missile defense sites near Tallinn, Estonia. By 1963, CIA and Air Force sharply disagreed over whether the sites were for defense against aircraft or part of a new, extensive ABM system. CIA took the former position, while Air Force, backed by DIA, took the latter.

The CIA position was strongly supported by Eugene Leggett, the chief of ORR's Defensive Missile Branch. Leggett eventually got McCone to support the CIA view in NIE 11-3-64, *Soviet Air and Air Defense Missile Capabilities Through Mid-1970.*[8] Leggett argued that the sites were too small and located in the wrong places to defend Moscow from a US ICBM attack. Subsequent satellite imagery during the next several years strengthened the CIA case, but not enough to rule out the ABM alternative. NIE 11-3-65, issued in November 1965, concluded that the Tallinn sites were probably for defense against a bomber attack using a new air-defense missile with a range several times that of the SA-2.[9] DIA and Air Force formally dissented, stating their position that the Tallinn and other associated sites were primarily for defense against ballistic missiles. The next three estimates, issued in 1966 through 1968 after McCone's departure, concluded on the basis of improved satellite photography that the system was for defense against an airborne attack using the new long-range SA-5 air defense missile.[10] The military services continued to dissent into the next decade, arguing that the SA-5s could be modified for an ABM role.

The Soviet Ground Forces Issue

Another major CIA dispute with DIA and the services that arose during the McCone era pertained to the size and strength of Soviet Bloc ground forces. The previously mentioned publication of NIE 11-14-62, *Capabilities of the Soviet Theater Forces*, in December 1962 triggered the dispute. The estimate stated that Soviet ground forces had a manpower strength of nearly 2 million men organized into 145 divisions, of which 80 were assessed to be at full strength and combat-ready. Before this estimate, McNamara's office was already raising questions about the size, strength, and capabilities of Soviet theater forces as well as the cost of maintaining them. The issue had major implications for both US and NATO defense budgets.

The NIE triggered a letter from McNamara to McCone questioning how the Soviets could achieve such strength with the resources available to them. The letter called for a joint CIA-DIA study to examine in detail all aspects of Soviet ground forces—including training, weapons, manning, and readiness—as well as the costs and economic feasibility of maintaining them. McCone's reply was drafted by Proctor and coordinated with Gen. Joseph F. Carroll, the head of DIA. In the letter the DCI formally established the joint panel and agreed to address the substantive issues that McNamara had raised. Proctor was then named the Agency co-chair of the joint panel.

Despite agreement for a joint panel, however, CIA's problems with DIA were only beginning. The major analytical issue involved—as with the previous bomber- and missile-gap controversies—was that CIA's military-economic costing efforts required cooperation with DIA and the services on basic military order-of-battle assessments for Soviet Bloc forces. Once again, this proved difficult because DIA was reluctant to have CIA challenge its Soviet military force assessments. At the same time, DIA lacked the capability to do its own economic and costing analysis of Soviet forces. However, Proctor was informed that DIA planned to establish its own Military Economic Research Branch, which it did in June 1963.[11]

Initially, DIA refused to cooperate with CIA, but after the intervention of both McCone and McNamara, a new DIA co-chairman was appointed, and the problems were resolved. The joint panel completed an interim report in September 1963, which was sent to McNamara. The report was also used as input to NIE 11-14-63, *Capabilities of the Soviet General Purpose Forces, 1963-69,* issued in January 1964. The report and the NIE focused on Soviet manpower strength and the number of ground force divisions. Compared to the 1962 NIE, the 1963 estimate lowered Soviet manpower strength from nearly 2 million to 1.6–.8 million, the number of line divisions from 145 to 110–140, and the number of combat-ready divisions from 60–80 to 75. It stated that Soviet forces were postured to withstand an initial attack and to go on the offensive to occupy strategically important areas of Western Europe. It also acknowledged the high level of uncertainty in the data, including the lack of firm information on unit strength, weapons and equipment, and readiness levels. No estimate of unit size was presented, except to note that even at full strength, Soviet divisions were considerably smaller than US divisions.

Shortly after the release of the NIE, McNamara acknowledged the success of the first phase of the panel's analysis but stressed the importance of the work still to be done. He hoped that further progress could be made on assessing the strengths and weaknesses of the Soviets as well as follow-on unit organization and equipment, production and inventory, and costing. In response, the panel undertook a second two-year study to prepare an inventory of equipment in the Soviet Army. The final report, issued in August 1965 after McCone's departure, concluded that the evidence was insufficient to quantify production and inventory of Soviet ground combat equipment and inventory within useful limits.

Nonetheless, the report raised hopes that improved satellite imagery would provide better information and help to close the intelligence gaps. This proved to be the case. In late 1967, the Ground Forces

Branch in ORR completed a detailed study of the Soviet Union's Belorussian Military District using new high-resolution satellite imagery. The study concluded that Soviet ground force divisions in rear areas were not equipped at full strength, and other units had either been misidentified or did not exist at all. Eugene Leggett, who had replaced Carl Erickson as chief of the Ground Forces Branch, and six other analysts were given merit awards for developing a new method to reduce uncertainties regarding the strength of Soviet ground forces that would have broad applications in the future.

Under McCone's leadership, CIA's role in strategic military analysis began to expand well beyond current intelligence production and support for national intelligence estimates. In particular, CIA began to provide much more extensive military intelligence support to the Pentagon's budget planning process as well as to arms control efforts by the new Arms Control and Disarmament Agency (ACDA), created by President Kennedy in September 1961. These new responsibilities led to two significant intelligence reorganizations within CIA.

The establishment of the DS&T in 1963 and continued demands for more intelligence support to policymakers stimulated new attention in the DI on further expanding its military analysis and costing efforts. D/ORR Guthe proposed enlargement of Proctor's Military-Economic Division into a Military Research Area consisting of two divisions: a Programs Division for costing and a Forces Division for military hardware. Cline approved the proposal but kept the word "economic" in the title to avoid provoking DIA and the military services. The expanded Military-Economic Research Area (MRA) was formally established in March 1964 with Proctor as chief and Inlow as deputy. It contained a Military Expenditures Branch, a Strategy and Trends Branch, a Free World Branch, and a Space and Support Branch in the Programs Division and Air, Naval, and Ground Forces Branches in the Forces Division along with Strategic Missile and Defensive Missile Branches.

DoD Customers

Proctor's enlarged MRA made significant contributions to a new intelligence product designed to meet the needs of DoD policymakers. At the request of Deputy Assistant Secretary of Defense Alain Einthoven, Sherman Kent initiated a new ONE report titled "Intelligence Assumptions for Planning" (IAP) in September 1963. The report was designed to provide the Pentagon with detailed projections of future Soviet weapon systems out to as long as 10 years. Prepared with DCI approval and with heavy input from ORR, these projections would then be used to make budget decisions on new US weapon systems under development. The initial IAP was released in July 1964. Unlike NIEs, the projections contained quantitative ranges (e.g. 50-70 percent) of the likelihood of individual new Soviet weapons appearing in the force. No attempt was made to choose a most likely number for any particular weapon system or to consider any economic or strategic constraints on a particular system entering the force.

The IAP report, which was renamed "National Intelligence Projections for Planning" (NIPP) in 1966, also contained a warning that the low- or high-side projections were highly unlikely to prove accurate in any given time frame. Nevertheless, Pentagon planners frequently used only the high-end projections for their budget decisions on individual US weapons programs. This caused some unease, and CIA officials consistently attempted to inject more realistic mid-range numbers into the projections. Regardless of their limitations from an intelligence standpoint, the IAP and the NIPP became important planning documents during the McNamara era, and their preparation continued to demand considerable time and effort from ORR's military analysts and economists.

As a result of the continued DoD demand for detailed Soviet weapons and force projections, along with associated costs, the military branches in MRA began in 1964 to prepare detailed reviews of Soviet weapons production going back to 1950 in support of the IAP and NIPP projections. To do so, the branches had already found that they had to undertake detailed estimates of the order of battle of all Soviet military units, including not only manpower strength but also all military hardware and equipment. These estimates included not only ground, air, naval, and eventually missile forces but support units as well. This proved to be a labor-intensive effort, particularly when changes and updates were needed. The analysts' efforts highlighted the need for a new, automated database.

At the same time, John Godaire's Military Expenditures Branch in MRA was applying advanced data processing (ADP) techniques to the detailed costing effort. Much of this effort was based on the order-of-battle inputs from the military forces branches. The branch project officer for the new ADP system was Noel Firth. The new system, which took several years to develop, was eventually titled the "Strategic Cost Analysis Model (SCAM)." By the mid-1960s, SCAM contained three major data files: one for manpower and order of battle, a second for expenditures for each military unit, and a third for the production and procurement of military hardware. Total costs and expenditures were done in both rubles and dollars, using conversion ratios derived from various sources, including comparisons to US military manpower and hardware costs. These costing efforts became an essential contribution to CIA's support to ONE's annual IAP and NIPP reports.[12]

Vance-McCone Agreement

Meanwhile, DIA informed CIA in July 1964 that it planned to increase its own military costing efforts in an attempt to achieve an independent analytic capability. In October 1964, DIA requested that ORR provide it with copies of the SCAM costing tapes critical to CIA's costing efforts. The basis for the request was the inability of DIA to meet its own departmental requirements for economic intelligence. Proctor was reluctant to do so, however, and DDI Cline subsequently informed DIA that at the request of the Pentagon, it was expanding its own research in military expenditures. In January 1965, McCone formally asked McNamara to centralize control of the military costing effort in CIA.

This request resulted in a memorandum that Deputy Secretary of Defense Cyrus Vance sent to McCone in February 1965. Subsequently known as the "Vance-McCone Agreement," it stipulated that CIA had the primary responsibility for studies pertaining to the cost and resource impact of foreign military and space programs. At the same time, the memorandum made clear that CIA would continue to provide DoD with necessary military-economic data to meet its own requirements. This key agreement established CIA's primacy in military-economic intelligence and prevented an expensive duplication of effort by DIA. By implication, it also affirmed McNamara's preference for CIA's strategic intelligence products in this area. One important measure of CIA's success in its military costing efforts and the SCAM database is that they endured for 30 years as the backbone of CIA's military-economic research effort and were still going strong at the Cold War's end.[13]

The Vance-McCone Agreement was one of the last major military intelligence issues that McCone was able to resolve between CIA and the Pentagon before President Johnson replaced him as DCI on 28 April 1965. McCone was never able to establish the same close intelligence relationship with President Johnson that he had developed with President Kennedy during the Cuban Missile Crisis. Johnson did not like regular intelligence briefings—he preferred to read the PDB by himself. McCone was also pessimistic about the growing US military involvement in Vietnam, and his views were not well received at the White House. His access to the President declined to the point where he decided it was time to leave. McCone's successor was retired Adm. William Raborn. At the same time, Richard Helms replaced General Marshall Carter as the DDCI.

Raborn Era

During Raborn's tenure as DCI, the DI remained heavily involved in various military intelligence issues. One was the growing importance of military analysis on China. In October 1964, China conducted its first nuclear weapon test. In December, the first Chinese ballistic missile submarine was detected on satellite imagery, and it soon became clear that China was producing its own MiG-21 fighter aircraft and SA-2 air defense missiles. The Pentagon turned to CIA for an assessment of China's strategic military potential. In response, in early 1965

ORR did a review of key military issues concerning China, which concluded that much intelligence—especially communications intelligence (COMINT) and satellite imagery—was not being exploited because few analytic resources were available and no research projects were under way. The issue of whether and when China could produce an ICBM was highly speculative. As a result of the increased interest in China, DDI R. Jack Smith in early 1966 proposed that more analysts be assigned to work on China. ORR followed up by creating a new China Branch in the Forces Division of MRA that began to undertake in-depth research on Chinese military issues.

Another growing concern during this period was nuclear proliferation and strategic military issues in noncommunist countries. ORR had established a Free World Branch in its Military-Economic Division in March 1963. It was soon tasked to do a crash study of France's nuclear weapons program.[14] The branch gradually expanded its research to include advanced weapons programs in other countries, including Egypt, India, Israel, and South Africa. Unlike analysts working on communist countries, the branch was able to draw on many open sources for information. The Free World Branch's primary customers were the White House and the State Department. Under John Paisley, who took over in early 1964, the branch also began doing cost analysis of defense programs in various Free-World countries.

Also during Raborn's tenure, CIA became increasingly caught up in the Vietnam conflict. US bombing raids over North Vietnam had begun in February 1965, and a large buildup of US forces began in April. Raborn became concerned about keeping informed about the situation, and in July 1965, he created a special Vietnam Task Force to be a focal point for CIA collection and analysis on the conflict. The head of the task force was soon given higher status as Special Assistant for Vietnam Affairs (SAVA). SAVA was located in OCI spaces, and many OCI and ORR analysts were assigned to work there. Raborn had already asked these offices to produce studies on war trends and battle statistics and the potential escalation of the conflict; SAVA's concerns grew to include Viet Cong organization and morale as well as Soviet and Chinese support to the North.

In addition to creating SAVA, Raborn asked Smith in February 1966 to put together an interagency group to watch for the potential deployment of surface-to-surface missiles to North Vietnam. Called the "Lookout Task Force," the group was run by John Hicks, who had become acting director of the Military Division of OCI in August 1965 when Bruce Clarke left to attend the National War College. After the imposition of extensive new collection efforts against the introduction of any type of surface-to-surface missiles to the North, including strategic, tactical, or coastal defense, Hicks was able to report by July 1966 that none were being deployed.

Helms Becomes DCI

Raborn had only a short one-year tenure as DCI; President Johnson replaced him with Richard "Dick" Helms in May 1966. During Raborn's period in office, several important changes had taken place within the DI. The first was the resignation of Guthe as head of ORR in late 1965 and his replacement with William Morell. The second was Cline's decision to leave his position as DDI in January 1966 and be replaced by R. Jack Smith, whom he had earlier made his acting deputy. Smith served in this position for the next five years. The third was Smith's decision to name Proctor as his deputy in March 1966. Proctor had left his position in ORR as head of MRA in June 1965 to serve in ONE; he was replaced by his deputy, Roland Inlow.

When R. Jack Smith became DDI in January 1966, one of his first moves was to remove the Office of National Estimates from his own control and place it under the DCI. Smith believed that by the mid-1960s under DCI McCone, NIEs had become substantially CIA products. To draft the estimates, ONE had become almost entirely dependent on the DI's political, economic, scientific, and military inputs. Smith thought that the estimates needed to be national intelligence products done under the direct authority of the DCI; Sherman Kent and Helms both agreed.[15]

The transfer of ONE to the DCI cleared the way for Smith's next priority, the creation of a single DI office to do military intelligence analysis.

The idea was not new. Proctor had proposed a single office in early 1962, which led up to the creation of the Military-Economic Division. Howard Stoertz and Smith had made the same recommendation that year while working in ONE. Guthe revived the idea in August 1963 soon after McCone had created the DS&T and moved OSI into the new directorate; Proctor of ORR, Smith of OCI, and Kent of ONE all supported the proposal. In both cases, DDI Cline was reluctant to create a single military intelligence office, presumably owing to fear of raising concerns in the Pentagon about a CIA challenge to DoD's intelligence authorities.

Smith had no such compunctions. He knew that the creation of a single office to focus on military analysis was a bold stroke, but after his five years' service in ONE, he believed that the military services were too driven by parochial interests to make objective judgments of strategic threats, and he thought the president was ill-served by such disregard for impartial assessments. In June 1966, Smith appointed Clarke, who had returned from the National War College, as his special assistant for special projects and asked him to undertake a broad review of strategic military intelligence in CIA. The problem was not whether a single military office was needed, but rather how it should be formed.

Clarke formally relinquished his position as chief of OCI's Military Division to Hicks and picked two analysts from the division to form his Military Study Group: Philip Waggener, chief of the division's Strategic Forces Branch, and Raymond Firehock from the division's Scientific and Technical Branch. The three labored for seven months on the task and produced a final report in February 1967.[16] The study began by defining military intelligence and then examined the role that CIA played in doing military analysis for policymakers. It discussed the legal justification for the effort, concluding that much duplication of effort on military intelligence existed among CIA, DIA, and the military services but such duplication was necessary and desirable. The reason cited was that the DCI has a unique responsibility for providing the president with the intelligence needed to ensure our country's national security, and that the president would have difficulty operating without input from CIA's independent military analysis.

The report then looked closely at military production in the DDI, focusing on ORR and OCI because they contained the most resources. After considering various alternatives, the study recommended that the DDI create a single office from the existing components of ORR and OCI that already focused on military research and analysis. The new office would consist primarily of the Military-Economic Research Area in ORR and the Military Division of OCI. To these would be added the Factory Markings Staff (FMS) from ORR and the small Military Branch of the China Division of OCI. The report specifically failed to include in the new office those ORR and OCI elements involved in intelligence analysis of Vietnam, primarily because of the potential disruption that might result to this high-priority intelligence support effort.

The study recommended that the new office be organized into three research divisions drawn from MRA: Strategic Forces Division, Theater Forces Division, and Programs Analysis Division. Most of OCI's Military Division would be put into a new Regional Analysis Division responsible for current intelligence reporting on military issues in communist countries as well as those Free-World countries having strategic military significance. The Regional Analysis Division would also assume the responsibility for current reporting on military-related scientific and technical intelligence on behalf of the DS&T. After assuring the DCI front office that the new office would not require additional money or manpower, Smith sent the study to DCI Helms in mid-June 1967. Smith proposed that the new office be named the Office of Strategic Research (OSR), avoiding the word "military" so as not to offend the Pentagon. He added that the new office would provide a single point in the DDI for managing the production of strategic military intelligence more effectively, including with ONE and the DS&T. Helms quickly approved, and OSR was formally established on 1 July 1967 with Bruce Clarke as director and Roland Inlow as his deputy.

OSR's mission was spelled out in its charter:

> *This office will be responsible for the production of substantive intelligence on strategic military and military-related problems of the Communist counties and additional countries as appropriate. It will combine the components in the Office of Research and*

Reports and the Office of Current Intelligence now working these topics. This reorganization will provide a single focal point for managing these resources more effectively and for contacts by the Office of National Estimates and the Directorate of Science and Technology.[17]

❖ ❖ ❖

Endnotes

1. Details on Smith's actions in the DI during this period are provided in Smith, *The Unknown CIA*, 145-164.

2. Clarke, interview with James Hanrahan, 25 April 2002.

3. See Peter Clement, "The Cuban Missile Crisis" in CIA, Directorate of Intelligence, 89-130 for details on the role of military intelligence during the crisis period.

4. Firth and Noren, *Soviet Defense Spending*, 34-97.

5. NIE 11-8-62, *Soviet Capabilities for Long-Range Attack*, 6 July 1962.

6. NIE 11-8/1-61, *Strengthened Deployment of Soviet Long-Range Ballistic Missile Forces*, 21 September 1961.

7. NIEs done during the McCone years are included in Steury, *Intentions and Capabilities*, 139-222. For a detailed discussion of McCone's problems with the Air Force on Soviet strategic military issues see Robarge, *John McCone as Director of Central Intelligence*, 229-238.

8. NIE 11-3-64, *Soviet Air and Air Defense Missile Capabilities Through Mid-1970*, 16 December 1964.

9. NIE 11-3-65, *Soviet Air and Air Defense Missile Capabilities*, 18 November 1965.

10. See NIE 11-3-66, *Soviet Strategic Air Missile Defenses*, 17 November 1966 and two other NIEs with the same title: NIE 11-3-67, 9 November 1967; and NIE 11-3-68, 31 October 1968.

11. Firth and Noren, *Soviet Defense Spending*, 37-38.

12. Ibid., 48–51.

13. Ibid., 37–38.

14. Parkinson and Potter, "Development of Strategic Research in CIA," 324.

15. Smith's actions on becoming DDI are covered in Smith, *The Unknown CIA*, 170-174.

16. The report is titled "Survey of Military Intelligence Production in the Intelligence Directorate" February 1967, Doc. ID 951480.

17. Memorandum for the Director of Support, "Establishment of a New Office Within the Intelligence Directorate," from R. J. Smith, Deputy Director for Intelligence, 23 June 1967.

❖ ❖ ❖

Chapter Three: 1967–71

The Early Years of OSR and the Transition to the Nixon Administration

Smith stated in his book, *The Unknown CIA*:

> *I picked Bruce Clarke Jr., a sharp aggressive man, to study the feasibility and advantages of combining the separate groups into a single office, and on the strength of the report, I created the Office of Strategic Research under Clarke's leadership. This was considered a bold stroke. By long-standing custom, and for a time, mutual consent, military affairs were held to be the exclusive province of the armed forces. Military intelligence was thought to be too arcane for mere civilians...Unfortunately for this concept, the military services throughout the 1950s and 1960s had consistently displayed an inability to make objective, dispassionate judgments regarding the strategic threat...For reasons easy to perceive, military intelligence analysts invariably leaned toward the worst case, the maximum conceivable threat...I knew that the President and the National Security Council (NSC) were ill-served by such work. It was time for CIA to assume the role in military affairs it had already established in the political and economic realms. The Office of Strategic Research constituted a statement to other intelligence agencies that CIA had a professional competence in strategic military affairs. Under Clarke, it soon became a strong voice in the field.*[1]

OSR was able to get off to a fast start because its senior leadership had considerable experience in military analysis and its components were transferred largely intact from ORR and OCI. Deputy Director Inlow had been the first chief of ORR's new Guided Missile Branch in 1956, and he became Proctor's deputy when the Guided Missile Task Force was formed in early 1960 and when the Military-Economic Division was created in 1962. He then took over the Military-Economic Research Area in 1965 when Proctor joined the ONE staff.

Inlow was Clarke's deputy until early 1969, when Inlow left OSR to become the second chairman of the Committee on Imagery Requirements and Exploitation (COMIREX). DCI Helms had established COMIREX in July 1967 as an IC organization to oversee the collection, processing, and exploitation of overhead imagery. At the same time, NPIC essentially became a joint community organization staffed with personnel from both CIA and DIA. To compensate for the change, the Imagery Analyst Service (IAS) was also created in July 1967 to provide direct imagery support to CIA; Howard Stoertz from ONE became its first leader.

OSR's Initial Organization

OSR was organized into four divisions (see chart, OSR 1967).[2] The new Programs Analysis Division (PAD) was headed by John Paisley, and his deputy was John Godaire. It had three branches: Cost Analysis, Military Expenditures, and Strategy and Trends. As mentioned earlier, Paisley had become chief of the Free World Branch in MRA in 1964, and before then, he had been the head of ORR's Electronic Equipment Branch since 1957. In mid-1966, he became chief of MRA's Programs Division with Godaire as his deputy, and both continued in these positions when OSR was created. Godaire had long experience as a military costing analyst in ORR. He became the first chief of the Military Economics Branch when it was created in 1953 and remained there during numerous ORR reorganizations until becoming Paisley's deputy.

The chief of the new Strategic Forces Division (SFD) was Robert Hastings; his deputy was Bill Baier. The division had three branches: Defensive Missiles, Offensive Missiles, and Space Systems. Hastings was the

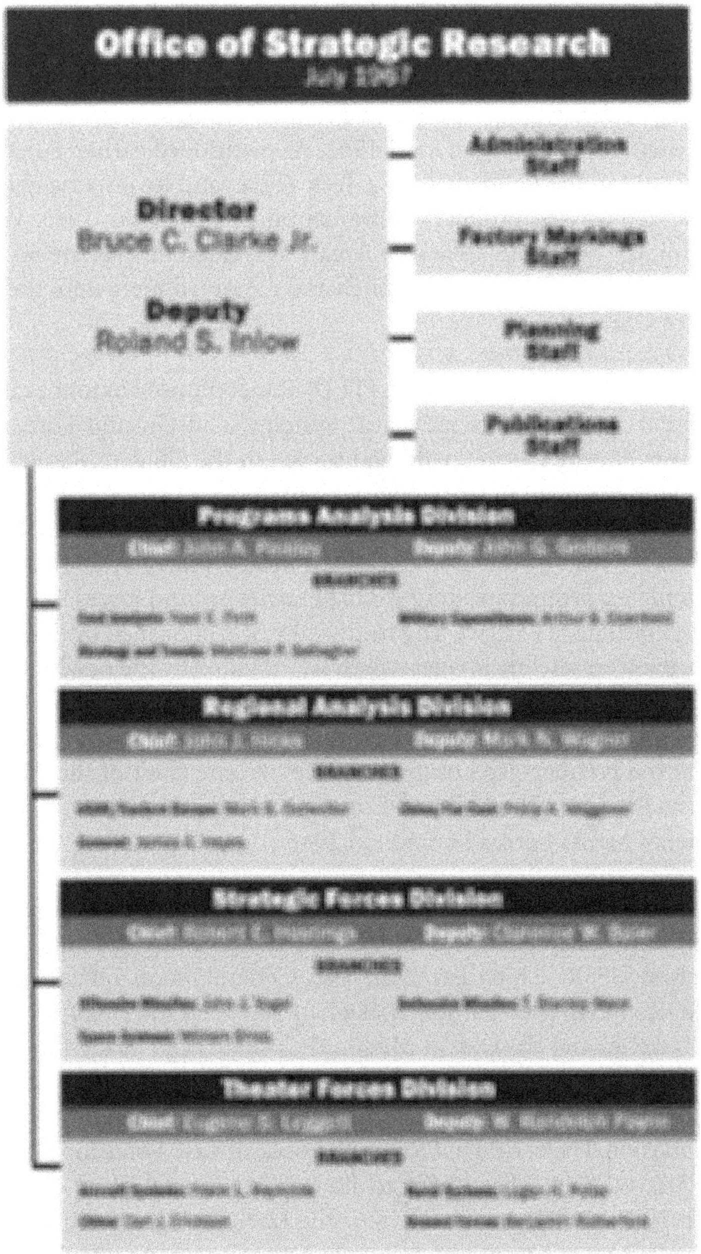
Office of Strategic Research
July 1967
Director
Bruce C. Clarke Jr.
Deputy
Roland S. Inlow
Administration Staff
Factory Markings Staff
Planning Staff
Publications Staff
Programs Analysis Division
Regional Analysis Division
Strategic Forces Division
Theater Forces Division

first chief of MRA's Forces Division when it was created in early 1964, and he remained there until the division was divided into two components at the creation of OSR. Prior to that, he had served in Proctor's Guided Missile Task Force from 1960 to 1962 and then as chief of the Military Programming. Branch in Proctor's Military-Economic Division when it was created in early 1962. As mentioned earlier, Baier had also served in the Guided Missile Task Force, and he became chief of the Guided Missile Production Branch under Proctor in 1962. When the Military-Economic Research Area was created in 1964, he became head of the Strategic Missiles Branch and remained there until the creation of OSR.

The new Theater Forces Division (TFD) was composed of four branches: China, Aircraft Systems, Naval Systems, and Ground Forces. Its chief was Eugene Leggett, who had served in the Guided Missile Task Force and was head of the Defensive Missiles Branch in MRA beginning in 1964 during the ABM missile controversy with the Air Force. He then led the Ground Forces Branch in MRA in early 1967 in time to complete a groundbreaking study of Soviet ground forces in the Belorussian Military District. The study—the first published by OSR—relied heavily on satellite imagery analysis provided by the newly created IAS. Leggett's deputy, Randy Payne, had helped ORR's Aircraft Branch to develop the methodology for estimating Soviet bomber production during the bomber-gap controversy. He became chief of the Aircraft Systems Branch in the Military-Economic Division in 1962 and deputy chief of MRA's Forces Division in 1966.

The chief of the new Regional Analysis Division (RAD) was John Hicks, and his deputy was Mark Wagner. The division had three branches: USSR, China/Far East, and General, soon renamed Free World. As mentioned earlier, Hicks had run the OCI situation room for Clarke during the Cuban Missile Crisis. He then headed the Military Division's Scientific and Technical Branch until 1965, when he took over from Clarke as division chief. While still heading the Military Division, Hicks led DCI Raborn's Lookout Task Force for Vietnam until August 1966, when he left to attend the National War College. In March 1967, DCI Helms reactivated the Lookout Task Force to watch for the introduction of any new Soviet-type weapons into Vietnam, this time with Hicks's deputy and acting division chief, Mark Wagner, in charge. Prior to this assignment, Wagner had been chief of the Strategic Forces Branch in the Military Division.

At the same time that OSR was created, ORR was renamed the Office of Economic Research (OER). It was headed by William Morell, who had led ORR beginning in December 1965. The removal of the Military Economic Research Area from ORR left the office with almost no one doing military-related analysis, with the exception of those working on the Vietnam conflict. A Vietnam Branch had been created in ORR in 1966. By 1967, the demand for economic and logistical intelligence on the conflict had risen so much that an Indochina Division had been created in OER. Its focus was primarily on economic and logistical intelligence on Indochina in support of SAVA. Although OSR was not directly involved in doing military analysis of the Vietnam War, Hicks continued to chair the Lookout Task Force, and OSR analysts continued to contribute to the task force's reports. The head of the Factory Markings Staff was Sidney "Wes" Finer, who had been assigned to lead the staff in mid-1966 before its transfer from ORR to OSR. The factory markings effort had a long history in ORR dating back to the Korean War.

1968 Annual Report

In September 1968, Clarke sent to DDI Smith what was to be the first of six annual reports done on OSR's activities and accomplishments during the previous fiscal year, which began on 1 October 1967.[3] The FY 1968 report's highlights included OSR's efforts to establish close working relationships with other Agency components that had a role in intelligence analysis on military subjects, including OSI and FMSAC in the DS&T and OER and OCI in the DI. Clarke also mentioned OSR's close analytic involvement with NPIC and IAS, both of which provided OSR with imagery support. Clarke then discussed OSR's major contributions to the estimative process, including 12 NIEs, most of which pertained to the Soviet Union, China, and other communist countries.

Clarke then focused on several of OSR's major analytic efforts. The first was the beginning of a joint study with DIA on the Soviet Union's capability to reinforce ground forces deployed against NATO in Western Europe. The study was requested by Secretary McNamara, who had been impressed by a report done the previous year on Soviet ground forces in the Belorussian Military District. The Ground Forces Branch in Theater Forces Division did the study with a great deal of imagery analysis from IAS. The Strategic Forces Division completed an exhaustive study of the largest Soviet joint forces exercise ever held in order to improve its understanding of Soviet strategic attack capabilities. The study used the full spectrum of intelligence sources—including technical collection, clandestine reports, and Soviet press—to analyze the significance of the exercise for Soviet strategy and tactics. Finally, the China Branch did a major study of the impact of the Cultural Revolution on Chinese strategic missile programs. The study concluded that internal turmoil and unrest had severely disrupted Chinese missile development and production.

Clarke next discussed the full spectrum of OSR's production efforts, including over 400 articles published in current intelligence publications and 56 in-depth intelligence memoranda and reports. He mentioned increased support to policymakers, including DoD, the State Department, and the Arms Control and Disarmament Agency, particularly on CIA's ability to monitor Soviet compliance with potential strategic arms limitation treaties. Clarke also mentioned OSR's support to CIA crisis task forces, briefing efforts, technical collection guidance, and liaison activities with US military allies. Next, he discussed OSR's application of computers to analytic problems and costing efforts and the reorganization required of the Programs Analysis Division to better support the efforts of the research divisions. He also covered OSR's enhanced efforts to provide better military training to its personnel, including attending DoD-sponsored weapons courses, visiting weapons plants and military installations, and setting up special training courses at NSA for OSR analysts. Clarke ended the report with a section on the outlook for OSR, including increased demands for intelligence on Soviet and Chinese military forces, as well as on North Korea and the Free World. He also mentioned the need to work more closely with State, DIA, and NSA and to continue to improve OSR's computer support and databases.

Bruce Clarke's Leadership Style

Clarke's initial annual report and those that followed give some indication about Clarke's personality and management style. Smith had described Clarke as having a sharp, aggressive personality, and the report makes clear that Clarke sought to please those higher up in his chain of command as well as to maintain good working relations with close associates. He also wanted the office to succeed in demonstrating its professional competence in military analysis to both its consumers and its critics, particularly in the Pentagon. He paid close attention to every major effort that OSR was involved in and how it managed its resources. He was conscious of the need to maintain and improve OSR's relationships with other CIA components as well as with other intelligence organizations.

Perhaps most important to troops in the trenches, Clarke cared much about his people. He had a legendary ability to remember the names and responsibilities of almost every analyst in OSR. He was a demanding boss but rewarded hard work and excellence. He insisted that no one could get an outstanding rating in a performance review unless he personally approved it. Clarke wanted the best analysts to be selected for advanced training and foreign travel, as well as for task forces and senior briefing opportunities. The higher that officers rose in the chain of command, the more they appreciated and learned from his management style. Many senior managers in OSR went on to even higher leadership positions inside and outside the Agency.

Clarke said that one of his goals for OSR was to ensure that he would have the best people in senior management positions five years down the road, so it was important to identify them early on.[4] He held regular weekend offsites with a cross-section of OSR personnel, from secretaries to division chiefs, so he could learn who they were and what they were doing. The most promising midlevel managers were sent to military service schools such as the Armed Forces Staff College for further training; more senior managers were sent to senior military schools such as the National War College or the Army War College. Clarke was very proud of the fact that many former OSR analysts—

such as Richard Kerr, Rae Huffstutler, Douglas MacEachin, and Frank Ruocco—went on to hold some of the most senior positions in CIA.

1969 Annual Report

Clarke's next annual report for fiscal year 1969 began with a reference to the August 1968 Soviet invasion of Czechoslovakia and its negative impact on the Johnson administration's efforts to begin strategic arms limitation talks with the Soviet Union.[5] It then focused on the change of administrations from President Johnson to President Nixon, which placed a heavy burden on OSR analysts because of the high demand for intelligence inputs for foreign policy decisionmaking from Henry Kissinger, Nixon's national security advisor. In particular, Kissinger initiated a new policy planning process, directed by the NSC staff, that mandated the drafting of detailed National Security Study Memorandums (NSSMs). Many of these required considerable intelligence inputs and the formation of working groups and committees to manage the process. Clarke said that he served as the CIA representative for several NSSMs, including one on US military posture chaired by the Defense Department and another on preparations for strategic arms talks with the Soviet Union chaired by ACDA.

Clarke mentioned that the Regional Analysis Division played a key role in current intelligence reporting during the prolonged buildup to the Soviet invasion of Czechoslovakia and that it also staffed the task force created in the wake of the invasion. The chief of the USSR Branch, R. Sams Smith, headed the task force, and one of its members, Douglas MacEachin, contributed heavily to its numerous situation reports. CIA came under heavy criticism for failing to warn of the invasion, but MacEachin, who would eventually become the DDI in the mid-1990s, rejected the claim. He subsequently pointed out that OSR had accurately reported Soviet military preparations and the force buildup, and that a Soviet intervention was a stated option in CIA reporting. Although he admitted that CIA had no reliable source of intelligence to report on Soviet military intentions, MacEachin believed that without such a source, policymakers were reluctant to admit that an invasion might happen. MacEachin characterized the episode as a classic case of policymakers' unwillingness to accept intelligence that contravenes current US policy.[6]

Clarke also mentioned several other key events and issues that demanded a great deal of analysts' time and effort. These included increased military clashes between China and the Soviet Union and hostile military actions by North Korea against US reconnaissance efforts, including the seizure of the *Pueblo* spy ship and the EC-121 shootdown. The Regional Analysis Division also continued to contribute to regular Lookout reports on Vietnam and to do preliminary assessments of the military highlights from each new satellite reconnaissance mission. Finally, it helped produce over 600 items for various current intelligence publications.

Regarding in-depth analysis, Clarke stated that OSR no longer drafted a single, large contribution to each new Soviet military estimate, as was done on the past. Instead, it generally made periodic inputs in the form of its own Intelligence Reports and Memorandums on key estimative subjects, and it also contributed in the form of National Intelligence Projections for Planning (NIPPs) still being done for the Defense Department. In all, OSR published 78 research studies, including 16 contributions to NIEs in 1969. These included a study of the likely pace of future Soviet ABM deployment, a detailed analysis of the production rates of Soviet Y-class nuclear ballistic missile submarines, a continued joint study with DIA and IAS of Soviet theater forces, a report on the Soviet buildup opposite China, and assessments of the Soviet Mediterranean squadron and Soviet tactical air forces. More attention was also given to China and North Korea, and the China Branch was split in two to cover both strategic and theater forces in both countries.

The Y-class submarine study was particularly important because it represented one of the few times in the late 1960s when OSR projected higher future force levels for a Soviet strategic weapon systems than the military services, in this case the Office of Naval Intelligence (ONI). ONI had disagreed with the CIA position, outlined in the 1965 NIE on Soviet strategic attack forces, that a new class of nuclear-powered ballistic missile submarine (SSBN) would probably be produced and deployed by 1968 and that it would probably carry as many as 12 improved ballistic missiles. However, satellite imagery in late 1966 revealed a new class of SSBN under construction, and this information was included in the 1966 NIE 11-8-66. Nevertheless, disagreement arose between CIA and ONI over future force levels. Logan Potter, the head of MRA's Naval Systems Branch in ORR, believed that the Soviets were striving for parity with the US Polaris SSBN program and would produce 35–45 Y-class submarines by the mid-1970s. ONI and DIA foresaw a more modest force of 15–25. The IC reached a compromise: 30 submarines. In the 1968 NIE, OSR got agreement that the Soviets most likely would have had a force of 35—50 Y-class SSBNs by the mid-1970s, each with 16 tubes and a new missile system. In fact, by 1973 the Soviets had produced 31 Y-class SSBNs and three lengthened variants, designated the "D-class."[7]

Clarke next addressed relations with other CIA components that had a role in analysis of military subjects. He stated that close relationships had been established with OSI and FMSAC as well as with OER and OCI, including the production of eight joint studies. He also mentioned the close relations with collectors, including the key part that OSR had in collection guidance and exploitation of satellite imagery done in conjunction with IAS and NPIC. He added that a closer rapport had been established with NSA as a result of continued training and visits, which had begun in 1968. Finally, Clarke discussed ongoing efforts to improve OSR's use of automatic data processing, including not only SCAM but QUIKTRAC.[a] QUIKTRAC was begun in 1968 as a major effort to transfer the entire database on ground forces to computer files to allow optimal manipulation and analysis. In 1969, the hope was to expand the concept to eventually include a comprehensive data bank of all Soviet and Chinese military forces.

Clarke did not mention in his 1969 annual report the controversy that CIA had had with the Nixon administration that year over the issue of whether the Soviets were seeking the capability to launch a first-strike nuclear attack on the United States. The United States was already deploying ICBMS with multiple independently targetable reentry vehicle (MIRV) warheads capable of striking more targets with a

a. SCAM refers to Soviet Cost Analysis Model, a CIA computer-based system to store Soviet military cost data and produce calculations of military expenditures. QUIKTRAC was a computer database developed to support analysis of Soviet Bloc and Chinese military forces and equipment.

single launch. The Pentagon argued that such a capability was needed to counter the Soviets' growing ABM system, which threatened the US defense strategy of "mutually assured destruction." Furthermore, because the United States lacked an extensive ABM program of its own, if the Soviets sought to deploy ICBMs with MIRVs, Washington would need to build an ABM system or risk a Soviet first-strike attack. The new Nixon administration was determined to get congressional approval for an expanded ABM program; Defense Secretary Melvin Laird took the lead on the issue.[8]

The 1968 NIE on Soviet strategic attack forces stated that testing of an SS-9 ICBM had been detected that was possibly a MIRV. The DS&T, led by Carl Duckett, subsequently concluded that the test was not a MIRV test because the warheads were not independently targetable and therefore the Soviets were not seeking a first-strike capability. Clarke and OSR concurred with this judgment. The Air Force disagreed, however, arguing that the evidence was not conclusive and that a Soviet intention to develop a first-strike capability in the absence of a US ABM system could not be ruled out. When CIA still maintained that the SS-9 was not MIRVed in an updated draft NIE 11-8-69, *Soviet Strategic Attack Forces*, 9 September 1969, Laird asked DCI Helms to remove the offending no-first-strike judgment. Helms did so, but the controversy was not over. DDI Smith was sent to the White House with the new head of ONE, Abbot Smith, to make the case to Kissinger, but the two men failed to persuade the national security advisor. Instead, Kissinger insisted that CIA give him the evidence on the SS-9 so the NSC staff could reach its own conclusions. OSR and FMSAC did a major study in response to Kissinger's concerns; the study concluded that the Soviets still lacked a MIRVed missile. As it turned out, the Soviet Union did not test a MIRVed SS-9 ICBM until five years later, in 1974.

A leadership change that took place in the OSR front office in early 1969 would bring a new face to the forefront. Roland Inlow left the deputy director position to become chairman of COMIREX, and Clarke replaced him with John Paisley, who was then chief of the Programs Analysis Division. Paisley was to remain the deputy director after Clarke left for the Pentagon and was replaced by Hank Knoche in September 1973. Paisley then retired from CIA in 1974, but he was called out of retirement in 1976 to help organize the "A-Team/B-Team" competitive analysis effort on Soviet military intentions approved by DCI George Bush.

1970 Annual Report

Clarke's 1970 annual report to the DDI was nearly twice as long as the first two.[9] In it, he announced a major reorganization and expansion of OSR to meet the ever-increasing demands for strategic intelligence support from the White House. The opening of strategic arms limitation talks (SALT) with the Soviets in the fall of 1969 had generated significant new intelligence requirements, including continued support to the NSC Verification Panel established the previous year. OSR was also tasked to support the newly created Defense Policy Review Committee (DPRC), which studied future US military force requirements. In addition, in early 1970, Helms tasked OSR to create a new President's Quarterly Report (PQR) on Soviet strategic forces in response to a White House request that CIA provide the administration with quarterly updates on the status of the Soviet strategic arsenal. Meanwhile, the volume of NSSM support continued to grow; OSR contributed to 11 new NSSMs on a wide variety of strategic issues, including not only those pertaining to the Soviet Bloc but North Korea and the Middle East as well. Finally, OSR continued to contribute heavily to the interagency working groups preparing National Intelligence Projections for Planning (NIPP) for DoD, which had begun during the McNamara era.

Clarke made it clear at the beginning of the report that direct support for policymakers was consuming most of OSR's resources. Support for the estimative process had become a lesser role. Such support was done mostly in the form of drawing from OSR's own intelligence reports that pertained to NIE subjects rather than as a single contribution to a particular estimate. Clarke went into considerable detail about the nature of this support and its demands on senior management. To oversee OSR's support to the SALT effort, Clarke in late 1969 had named Bill Baier as his special assistant for strategic arms talks. Baier, who had been the deputy chief of the Strategic Forces Division, held that position for the next two years; he soon became the Agency-wide coordinator for SALT support.

The bulk of Baier's work centered on the Verification Panel, which had become the central study group for SALT policy decisions. Four major assessments were done concerning SALT; other studies were done on MIRV and ABM issues. When the talks began in Helsinki in November 1969, a team of three DI analysts, led by Robert Hewitt of OSR, was sent to provide intelligence support to the US delegation. Meanwhile, Clarke became the DCI's representative to a Backstopping Committee established in Washington to provide daily policy support to the Helsinki delegation. Within OSR, a special staff was created to provide intelligence support to both the Helsinki and Washington efforts.

In early 1970, Clarke was named as the CIA representative to a new working group established to support the Defense Program Review Committee effort. The group prepared studies of key issues affecting decisions on future US military postures. The DPRC, chaired by Kissinger, included a senior representative from the State and Defense Departments and the Office of Management and Budget, the chairmen of the Joint Chiefs of Staff and the Council of Economic Advisors, and the DCI.

The nature of OSR's participation in the NSSM process varied widely. OSR played a significant role in two NSSMs and made major contributions to three others. For NSSM-84, *Alternative US Strategies and Forces for NATO*, Clarke was co-chairman of a CIA working group that drafted a four-part assessment of the Soviet and Warsaw Pact threat to NATO. For NSSM-9, *Mutual and Balanced Force Reductions Between NATO and the Warsaw Pact*, Clarke represented CIA at meetings of the steering committee, and OSR officers participated in subgroups on verification, options, strategic implications, and databases. OSR drafted major contributions to NSSM-81, *US Arms Policy Toward Israel*, and NSSMs-57 and -58 on civil defense and continuity of government.[10]

Clarke stated that the main purpose of the OSR reorganization, which took effect in January 1970, was to create a new division to focus on the growing military potential of Communist China and the growing threat from North Korea. The new unit, the Asian Communist Forces Division, was headed by Louis Sandine. It contained two branches: Strategic Forces and Theater Forces. During its first year, the division was involved in numerous important research activities. One was an in-depth study of Chinese forces in Shenyang Military Region, which was produced with extensive support from NPIC and IAS. It became an important contribution to NIE 13-3-70, *Communist China's General Purpose and Air Defense Forces.*[11] CIA used the format of the study to begin a joint project with DIA to examine the ground forces in all seven of China's military regions.

The division also worked closely with NPIC to do a methodical search of China's entire rail network for signs of strategic missile deployment, much as was being done in the Soviet Union. Other studies included a close look at China's growing TU-16 jet medium-bomber force, analysis of China's air defense and militia forces, and a report on the Chinese navy's coastal defense and submarine forces. Finally, the division contributed to a new biweekly report the White House requested on Sino-Soviet relations. The report—done jointly by OSR and OCI—contained military and political updates on the status of the growing border dispute between the Soviet Union and China.

Clarke added that at the same time that the Asian Communist Forces Division was formed, the research and analysis on the Soviet Bloc—which had formerly been done in the in the old Theater and Strategic Forces Divisions—came under the purview of the new Soviet and East European Forces Division. The new division was headed by Carl Erickson. The branches in the divisions were also restructured according to the major missions of the forces involved rather than by branch of service. The new branches included a Strategic Attack Branch, a Strategic Defense Branch, a Land Warfare Branch, and a Naval Operations Branch.

The Strategic Attack Branch—which was heavily involved in the SALT support effort—also completed numerous research studies, including several on Soviet ICBM deployment, one on Soviet peripheral missile forces, and another on the SSBN force. The Strategic Defense Branch produced reports on the growing Soviet ABM system around Moscow and the Hen House missile detection radars on the Soviet Union's periphery. It also did studies of production rates for the new Foxbat interceptor aircraft and future Soviet ASW capabilities and force levels.

Clarke stated that the major accomplishment of the Land Warfare Branch in 1970 was the completion of a comprehensive study of the Warsaw Pact Forces facing NATO. The study, which was based on research done over the previous two years, assessed the size and organization of Warsaw Pact forces as well as their doctrine and capabilities. OSR also continued to work jointly with DIA on a study of Soviet ground forces, which helped resolve some of the basic disagreements within NATO about Soviet ground force capabilities. Research was also begun for an in-depth analysis of military forces in Eastern Europe, including Poland, Czechoslovakia, East Germany, Hungary, and Bulgaria.

Clarke also detailed the current intelligence reporting done during the year in the Regional Analysis Division. He restated his strong belief that although substantive overlap existed between analysts in the division and those in the three research divisions, the separation of functions between current intelligence reporting and in-depth research was beneficial to both. Current intelligence analysts needed to have daily contact with their counterparts inside and outside CIA to prepare and coordinate items for the Central Intelligence Bulletin, CIA's daily intelligence report. Often working closely with OSI, FMSAC, and ONE. OSR analysts also prepared intelligence briefings for senior CIA officials to present to policymakers and congressional committees on Soviet and Chinese military issues. Finally, they did preliminary assessments of regular satellite reconnaissance missions, issued monthly Lookout Committee reports, and staffed crisis task forces when necessary.

Clarke next discussed the work of the Programs Analysis Division. He stated that its military-economic analysis was increasingly important to policymakers making decisions on key military programs and that in response to a presidential request, a special report was prepared on the 1970 Soviet defense budget and spending trends for major weapons programs. Work had also begun on estimating Chinese defense spending, including a report on the value of the previous production of military equipment and the first estimate of Chinese military expenditures for R&D. He added that continued improvements were being made to various OSR data bases, including SCAM and QUIKTRAK.

Clarke ended his 1970 report with a summary of OSR's production statistics during the first three years of its existence. He highlighted the increased number of research publications being done, especially those on Asian Communist forces. These included intelligence reports and memorandums as well as formal contributions to NIEs and NSSMs and to the SALT delegation. Overall, the number of research products increased to 93 in 1970, an increase of nearly 20 percent compared to the previous year and nearly 37 percent compared to 1968. By area, 65 percent of the publications focused on the Soviet Bloc, of which 18 percent focused on military policy and economics, 22 percent on strategic forces, and 25 percent on conventional forces. Another 21 percent of the production concerned Communist China and Asia, of which 3 percent covered military policy and economics, 7 percent missile forces, and 11 percent conventional forces. The remaining 14 percent of OSR's research products were devoted to Free-World military issues. Finally, Clarke mentioned that OSR continued to contribute a high volume of articles to CIA's current intelligence publications, including over 400 to the Current Intelligence Bulletin and nearly 80 to the two weekly publications.

Clarke clearly believed that after three years of OSR's existence, the office had justified the rationale for its creation. Furthermore, by pointing out the heavy demands for military intelligence support to policymakers from Kissinger and the new Nixon administration, Clarke was implying that without OSR, CIA would have had difficulty responding effectively. He did not mention substantive problems or intelligence disputes with the Nixon administration or within the Intelligence Community. He focused on the close relationships that OSR had developed with its intelligence partners inside and outside CIA but avoided mentioning any major coordination issues or problems. Instead, Clarke stressed OSR's accomplishment in his reports and admitted that much remained to be done.

Clarke worked hard to maintain good working relations with his DS&T and DI division counterparts, who by 1970 included Donald Chamberlain of OSI, David Brandwein of FMSAC, William Morell of OER, and Richard Lehman of OCI. Nevertheless, any OSR military analyst can attest to the fact that despite Clarke's efforts, coordination of current intelligence articles and research reports inside CIA was not always easy.

If the item had technical, economic, or political implications, analysts in either OSI, FMSAC, OER, or OCI would want to have their say. It was often easier to coordinate current intelligence items outside CIA with State/INR and DIA then it was to coordinate them internally, including with OSR counterparts in the research divisions. Research reports did not need external coordination, but that did not make internal coordination any easier. Clarke found out early on that even ONE could be a problem if a new OSR research report diverged from a previous estimative judgment. Clarke had to get Sherman Kent to agree that OSR had the right, as part of CIA, to publish its own departmental intelligence assessments and that differences could be worked out in the process of producing the next national intelligence estimate.[12]

❖ ❖ ❖

Endnotes

1. Smith, *The Unknown CIA*, 172-173.
2. "OSR Organization and Key Personnel," 7 July 1967.
3. "OSR Annual Report for Fiscal Year 1968," September 1968.
4. Clarke, interview with James Hanrahan, 25 April 2002.
5. "OSR Annual Report for Fiscal Year 1969," August 1969.
6. MacEachin, Douglas J., "Predicting the Soviet Invasion of Afghanistan: The Intelligence Community's Record," 15 April 2007. www.cia.gov.
7. CIA, NIE 11-8-66, *Soviet Capabilities for Strategic Attack*, 20 October 1966 and NIE 11-8-68, *Soviet Capabilities for Strategic Attack*, 3 October 1968.
8. The SS-9 MIRV controversy is discussed in Helms, *A Look Over My Shoulder*, 385-388; and Smith, *The Unknown CIA*, 205-209.
9. "Office of Strategic Research Annual Report, Fiscal Year 1970," August 1970.
10. A complete list of all NSSMs done during the Nixon administration from 1969-1974 with dates of publication can be found at: fas.org/irp/offdocs/nssm-nixon/index.html.
11. NIE 13-3-70, *Communist China's General Purpose and Air Defense Forces*, 7 June 1970.
12. Clarke, interview with James Hanrahan, 25 April 2002.

❖ ❖ ❖

Chapter Four: 1971–73

Clarke's Last Three Years as Director of OSR and the End of the Helms Era

A New Estimative Format

By early 1971, OSR was running at full steam to satisfy the military intelligence demands of the Nixon administration. The reorganization of the office announced in early 1970 was having a positive impact on OSR's ability to meet the increasing requirement from Kissinger and the NSC for more detailed analytic products, including national intelligence estimates. This was an outgrowth of the Nixon administration's dissatisfaction with NIE 11-8-69 on Soviet strategic forces, issued in September 1969 and the first done for the new President.[1] To prepare for the next NIE in the series, NIE 11-8-70, DDI Smith conferred directly with Kissinger and the NSC staff about a new estimative format. The requirement was not only for detailed facts and judgments but also for the reasoning behind the conclusions, consideration of alternative outcomes, and elaboration of any differences of opinion.[2]

When Smith gave the feedback to ONE about the new estimative format, ONE Chairman Abbot Smith strongly resisted. After the DDI informed the DCI of the problem, Helms gave drafting authority for the next Soviet strategic estimate (NIE 11-8-70) directly to the DDI. ONE continued to have the responsibility for Community coordination, however. OSR analysts, along with others in OSI and FMSAC, were given the responsibility for drafting major portions of the new estimate. Although the NIE took much longer to prepare, the payoff was evident. In particular, President Nixon sent a letter to Helms commending him and the entire Intelligence Community for NIE-11-8-70 on Soviet strategic forces. The President found "particularly useful" such elements as "the frequent sharply defined, clearly argued discussions of various contested issues...the alternative force models based on explicit differences in underlying assumptions...the quantitative detail for each model."[3]

Helms replaced ONE Chairman Smith with John Huizenga in early 1971, and the new estimative format and drafting process were adopted for future military NIEs. The stated intent of the changes was to make NIEs more useful to the President and the National Security Advisor to facilitate their decisionmaking. As a result, OSR and OSI were assigned responsibility for drafting NIEs on Soviet and Chinese military forces. Clarke stated that the emphasis was on detailed analysis and explicit statements and that, while the final drafts were of greater length than was customary in the past, policymakers were better able to judge for themselves the quality of CIA's knowledge and conclusions.[4]

OSR's Expansion

By early 1971, OSR had grown to about 190 positions despite CIA's tight budget constraints.[5] The front office, in addition to Clarke and Paisley, included Robert Hewitt as executive officer and T. Stanley Mace as special assistant for the SALT talks (see chart, "OSR 1971," opposite.) The Programs Analysis Division was then headed by Noel Firth, with Mark Boerner as Firth's deputy. The division contained four branches: Cost Analysis, Military Economic Planning, Strategic Evaluation, and Technical Resources. The Asian Communist Forces Division, headed by Lou Sandine and Clarence Baier, contained separate branches for Strategic Forces and Theater Forces in the region.

The Soviet and East European Forces Division—by far the largest in OSR—was headed by Carl Erickson, with Randy Payne as his deputy. The division had two designated senior analysts to coordinate responses to policy requests: James Hayes for Strategic Forces and John Bird

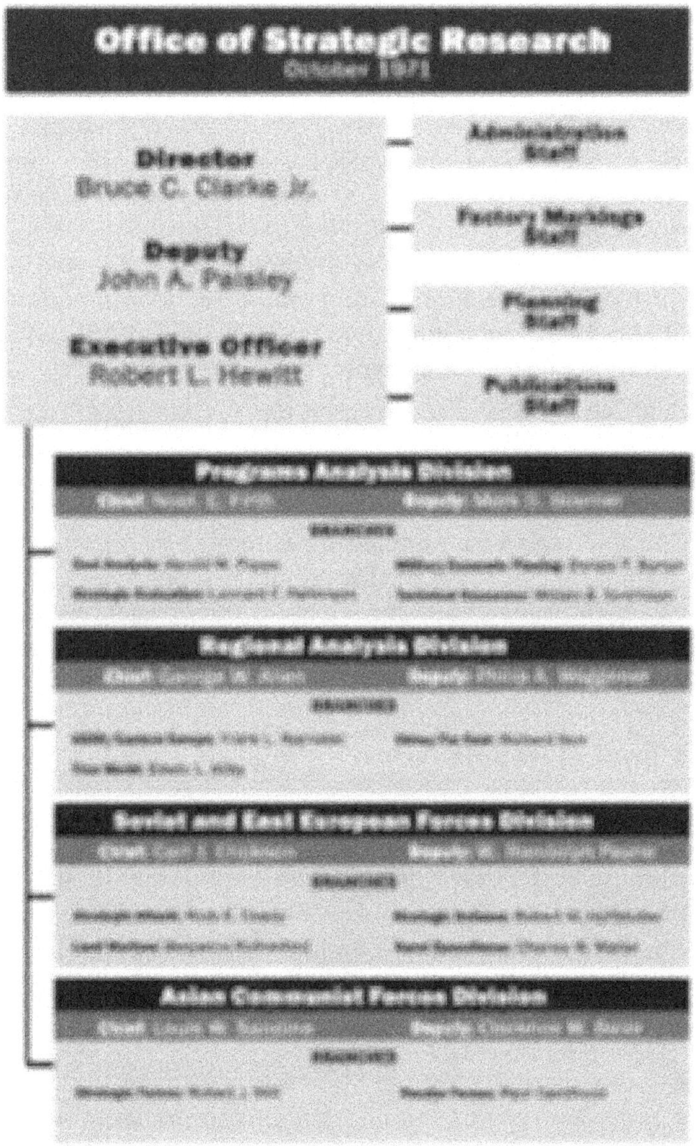
Office of Strategic Research
October 1971
Director
Bruce C. Clarke Jr.
Deputy
John A. Paisley
Executive Officer
Robert L. Hewitt
Administration Staff
Factory Markings Staff
Planning Staff
Publications Staff
Programs Analysis Division
Regional Analysis Division
Soviet and East European Forces Division
Asian Communist Forces Division

for Theater Forces. It had four branches: Strategic Attack, Strategic Defense, Land Warfare, and Naval Operations. Rae Huffstutler was the chief of the Strategic Defense Branch, his first management position in OSR.

Finally, the Regional Analysis Division (RAD) was headed by George Allen, with Philip Waggener as his deputy. It had three branches: China/Far East, Free World, and USSR/Eastern Europe. The China/Far East Branch was led by Richard Kerr; as with Huffstutler, it was Kerr's first management position in OSR. Kerr eventually rose to become the DDCI in 1989 under DCI William Webster. Allen is a good example of the high caliber of senior managers whom Clarke was able to attract to OSR. Allen had had a long career as a military analyst in the US Army and was considered an expert on Vietnam. He joined CIA in 1963 and was soon sent to Saigon as a DDI intelligence analyst until 1966. He then became the deputy to the special assistant for Vietnam affairs, George Carver, from 1966 to 1969. Allen joined OSR in early 1970 and became chief of the Regional Analysis Division. He left OSR in late 1972 to replace Howard Stoertz as head of the IAS until 1976. He subsequently held various other senior positions in CIA—including as director of the Center for the Study of Intelligence—until his retirement in 1979.

1971 Annual Report

Clarke's annual report to the DDI for fiscal year 1971 was sent to DCI Helms and to DDI Edward Proctor, who had replaced R. Jack Smith as DDI in May 1971. In his cover note, Clarke expressed his delight that Proctor had been appointed to the position because of the major role he had played in the creation of OSR. Clarke also included a cover note to R. Jack Smith, asking him to read the report before he (Smith) departed his position as DDI later that year.

Clarke began the report by noting that OSR's work was then largely shaped by senior officials' need for detailed assessments of the military capabilities of the Soviet Union, China, and other communist countries. Almost half of the report addressed the policy support role, while the remainder highlighted the work of OSR's major components. Clarke noted that the Nixon administration had created several mechanisms to develop policies on matters affecting national military programs. These included the National Security Study Memorandum process, the Defense Program Review Committee (DPRC), and separate verification panels for SALT and MBFR. The DCI represented the Intelligence Community in these forums; his staff was composed of senior CIA officials who led major components.

Clarke noted that he was the DCI's representative on the DPRC Working Group, which prepared intelligence input and reviewed the issues to be discussed under Kissinger's chairmanship. OSR provided support for three general areas of DPRC analysis. One was a major study of the survivability of US strategic forces, which required an analysis of the Soviet ASW threat to the US SSBN force. The others were the threats to the US strategic bomber fleet and the US land-based strategic missile force.

Clarke added that the responsibility for coordinating all planning and intelligence support pertaining to SALT within CIA was done by a DI-DS&T staff located in OSR and headed by Baier. He stated that the staff had completed 41 interagency studies for the SALT Verification Panel in 1971 and that when negotiation sessions were under way in Helsinki or Vienna, daily updates were provided to CIA representatives at those locations. In addition, the Soviet and East European Forces and Program Analysis Division did 16 basic SALT support studies on such issues as verification measures and the Soviet ICBM force buildup.

OSR contributed to seven NSSMs during 1971, including ones looking at the growing Soviet military presence worldwide. The heaviest demand for analysis was for NSSM-92, *Mutual and Balanced Force Reductions Between NATO and the Warsaw Pact*, and NSSM-69, *US Strategy and Forces for Asia*. In addition, much work was required in support of NSSM-84, *Alternative US Strategies and Forces for NATO*. Other NSSMs included ones on the Arab-Israeli military balance and US strategy in the Indian Ocean and the Caribbean.

Clarke stated that OSR took the lead in drafting four NIEs on the Soviet Union. These included ones on Soviet strategic attack and strategic defense capabilities as well as Soviet forces for operations in Eurasia and the uses of Soviet military power in distant areas. In addition, OSR headed the DDI-DDS&T-ONE drafting team for NIE 13-8-71 on China's strategic attack forces. Clarke added that OSR did all four issues of the President's Quarterly Report on Soviet Strategic Forces during 1971 with support from the Office of Basic and Geographic Intelligence (OBGI), FMSAC, OSI, and ONE. He noted that the establishment of a Soviet nuclear submarine support facility in Cuba in late 1970 led to considerable intelligence demands from the NSC staff, resulting in a daily situation report produced for a six-week period ending in early November 1970. Finally, the NSC and the State Department became concerned about the increased deployment of Soviet strategic air missile (SAM) sites in the Egyptian cease-fire zone opposite Israel in late 1970. This led to the creation of an interagency task force that produced a number of special assessments and memoranda on the situation, as well as briefings for Kissinger and the State Department.

The next section of Clarke's annual report addressed OSR's independent intelligence production. Clarke noted that current reporting remained about the same as the previous year but that research production had fallen off nearly 40 percent, primarily because of the heavy burden of direct policy support in response to NSC requests. Clarke always strongly supported basic intelligence research and production on subjects not always in high current demand as a way to build greater analytic knowledge and expertise. He thus began a semiannual review of OSR's research program to set production priorities a year ahead. OSR also became more selective in how it used its analytic resources and looked for ways to become more productive. Clarke transferred the responsibility of producing the National Intelligence Projections for Planning for DoD to DIA, and OSR sought to make even greater use of advanced data processing to help free analysts from having to do manual storage and manipulation of data.

Clarke stated that in addition to traditional studies of the capabilities of Soviet Bloc military forces, the Program Analysis Division was doing more work on Soviet strategic doctrine and planning and on Chinese defense expenditures. Noteworthy was a comprehensive study of Soviet defense spending for the years 1962–1971. The subject was becoming increasingly controversial, however, particularly when compared to US defense costs and programs. A serious DoD challenge to OSR's costing methodology would soon prove inevitable. Finally, Clarke noted that two analysts were working full time on the history of military analysis at CIA.[a, 6]

Clarke strongly believed that analysis should drive intelligence collection priorities. The annual report that Clarke produced each year had a section on collection and exploitation support. In Clarke's opinion, a good military analyst should not only know sources but also know how to provide collection guidance on needs and priorities and maintain a close relationship with collection counterparts. In the annual reports, Clarke mentioned OSR's heavy reliance on satellite photography, signals intelligence, and human reporting as key intelligence sources; he also highlighted the need to guide collection and exploitation by working closely with the collection agencies and managers. These included NPIC, IAS, and COMIREX for satellite photography, the SIGINT Committee and NSA for signals intelligence, and the Clandestine Services for human intelligence.

In the FY 1971 annual report, Clarke renamed the final section "data collection and processing" and emphasized the need for better data processing to make analysts' exploitation of the increasing volume of photographic and SIGINT material easier and more effective. He also mentioned the intensified efforts to use computers and ADP applications to handle both collection and analytic databases. Finally, he mentioned the increased use of SCAM—a computational rather than a storage and retrieval system—to generate the detailed cost data for OSR's estimates of Soviet defense expenditures. These estimates were used for alternative force models in the annual NIEs on Soviet strategic attack and strategic defense forces.

a. Although never published, the draft of this study by Logan Potter and Len Parkinson has been an invaluable source for this history.

CENTRAL INTELLIGENCE AGENCY

1972 Highlights

The year 1972 was momentous for OSR because it was the fifth anniversary of the office. At a ceremony on 23 June 1972 to celebrate the event, Clarke recounted the meeting that he and R. Jack Smith had had with DCI Helms to get Helms's approval for OSR's creation. Clarke said that the meeting lasted only two and a half minutes. Helms was very busy with the next year's budget; soon after the meeting began, Helms checked the time and asked, "How much more is this going to cost me?" Clarke answered, "Not a cent more," and Helms responded, "Okay, go to it." Helms could not attend the event, but he sent a note "To the People of OSR" in which he stated: "OSR's voice is heard throughout the government where national security matters are discussed. Your views are respected and your analysis is used with confidence." (See the full note on page 63.)

The year was also significant because of two major foreign policy achievements of the Nixon administration: the opening of relations with China, signified by the President's visit there in February 1972; and the signing of an ABM Treaty and an interim agreement on offensive weapons, termed "SALT I," during Nixon's subsequent trip to Moscow in May 1972. The ABM Treaty limited each country to two deployment sites. The Soviets chose to protect Moscow, while the United States built only one site to protect an ICBM launch facility. The interim agreement froze the number of deployed strategic missiles in each country, including ICBMs and SLBMs. The United States would be permitted 1,054 ICBMs and 710 SLBMs, the Soviet Union 1,607 ICBMs and 750 SLBMs. Both sides would be allowed to replace older missile systems and launchers with newer ones. OSR had played a key role in providing intelligence support for the opening of US relations with China as well as US-Soviet agreements. Both would result in new demands for military intelligence support from CIA, primarily to monitor treaty compliance and verification.

Clarke's 1972 annual report was the longest of the six he authored, primarily because he also reviewed key developments in OSR during the previous five years.[7] Clarke sent out 40 copies with signed cover notes; the first 16 contained personal comments. The first few of those included DCI Helms, DDI Proctor, Executive Director William Colby, and DDS&T Duckett. The next notes went to Director of FBIS Henry Knoche, Deputy Director for Operations (DDO) Thomas Karamessines, Director of Domestic Contact Service (DCS) James Murphy, and Director of National Estimates John Huizenga. The rest of the notes went to the heads of office-level organizations in the DI and DS&T, including David Brandwein in FMSAC, Donald Chamberlain in OSI, Arthur ("Art") Lundahl in NPIC, Howard Stoertz in IAS, Richard Lehman in OCI, Maurice Ernst in OER, John King in OBGI, and John Iams in the Office of Computer Services (OCS).

Clarke began the report with a short introduction about the changing environment in which OSR then operated compared to 1967. His four main points were: the office had become heavily involved in direct intelligence support to the NSC and policy forums such as the DPRC and the SALT and MBFR Verification Panels; new imagery and signals collection programs were providing major improvements in information on military matters; US and Soviet military competition on both land and sea had become worldwide in scope; and China had acquired strategic attack capabilities. Clarke stated that these developments validated and strengthened the original requirement that led to OSR's creation.

Clarke then provided a review of the year in brief. In addition to the NSC support effort on defense planning and arms control efforts, he highlighted the preparation of new background studies on China and the Soviet Union in preparation for the presidential visits to Peking and Moscow in 1972. He also listed several crisis areas during the previous year that had required significant current intelligence reporting. These included a Chinese leadership crisis in October 1971, the visit of a Soviet naval squadron to Cuba in November 1971, a rise in military tensions between Israel and Egypt, and the outbreak of war between India and Pakistan in December 1971.

On policy support, Clarke stated that about one third of the 150 NSSMs done for the NSC to date had required substantial OSR input and participation. In all, OSR participated in 18 NSSMs in FY 1972—more than double the number for the previous year. These included such diverse topics as military cooperation with France, the Law of the Sea,

US-UK nuclear relations, and the continuity of US government. The key ones were NSSM-69 on US strategy and forces for Asia, which was still being drafted, and NSSM-92 on MBFR, which was demanding increasing resources. Nixon and Soviet leader Leonid Brezhnev had agreed at the Moscow summit in May 1972 to begin formal MBFR talks the following year, and preparations for the negotiations were accelerated.

DCI Helms, in response to the signing of the SALT I ABM and interim treaties, had established a SALT Monitoring Steering Group composed of the directors of DIA and NSA, CIA's deputy director for intelligence, and State's head of intelligence. DDCI Vernon Walters was named chairman of the group, and Howard Stoertz of IAS was appointed special assistant to the DCI for SALT and head of a SALT intelligence working group. George Allen, who by then was OSR's special assistant for SALT support, subsequently replaced Stoertz as head of IAS in November 1972.

Clarke then detailed OSR's continuing heavy support to the NIE process. He focused on the fact that the Programs Analysis Division continued to provide the costs sections for all major military estimates as well as for two upcoming NIEs, *Issues and Options for Soviet Military Policy* and *Soviet Military Research and Development.*[8] As a result of these efforts, Clarke stated that the Director of DIA, General Donald Bennett, and DIA's director of estimates, General Daniel Graham, were now challenging the validity of CIA's work and CIA's contributions to NIEs. They expressed concern that CIA estimates had understated Soviet defense spending in the previous few years, and they called for a conference of nongovernment experts to examine the issue. In response, DDI Proctor sent a note to Helms requesting that the DCI establish a panel of recognized outside experts to examine CIA's methodology. Helms agreed, but the panel would not be fully staffed for another year. The first meeting of what became the Military-Economic Advisory Panel (MEAP) took place in April 1973; its first report was not issued until July 1974.[9]

Clarke concluded the entire second half of the 1972 annual report with a review and update of OSR's production during the previous five years. OSR's current reporting was achieved primarily through contributions by the Regional Analysis Division to OCI's periodicals, including the President's Daily Brief, the Current Intelligence Bulletin, and the Current Intelligence Weekly Review. These included current intelligence items that OSR produced on behalf of the DS&T. In addition, the division staffed various task forces, including one on the Indo-Pakistan War; wrote military briefings for the DCI; and contributed to periodic reports that other DDI offices prepared.

Clarke also went into considerable detail about OSR's research publications, which were produced by the Soviet and East European Forces, Asian Forces, and Program Analysis Divisions. He pointed out that in 1972, as in 1971, OSR had published fewer research products than in previous years because of the heavy burden of contributions to NSSMs, NIEs, and other policy support documents. Nevertheless, OSR's own intelligence reports and memorandums tended to be more comprehensive, and hence longer than policy support documents. In 1972 the number of printed pages for OSR reports reached an all-time high: 2,500. Clarke also pointed out that OSR's research on the Soviet military was increasingly focused on qualitative improvements rather than on quantitative ones and that more research was being done on Soviet military policy and doctrine, command and control, and force readiness. He then detailed studies by each branch in the Soviet and East European Forces Division as well as those done in the Programs Analysis Division.

Clarke stated that military research on Communist China and North Korea focused on providing more detail on force levels and deployments, including doing an in-depth analysis of Chinese ground forces with DIA. Studies were also completed on the Chinese air, naval, and strategic missiles forces and on the North Korean Air Force. In OSR's first five years, the percentage of research studies that OSR did on the Soviet Union and Eastern Europe accounted for about 70 percent of the office's total production. China and other communist countries in Asia accounted for 20 percent of production, and other countries about 10 percent.

The last major section of the 1972 report focused on data collection and processing. Clarke noted that during the previous five years, OSR had become the major CIA user of satellite imagery and that the volume of imagery had increased significantly in 1972 with the advent of the new KH-9 system, which collected high-resolution imagery over a wide area. This development resulted in closer collaboration on collection and exploitation with NPIC and IAS. In addition, NSA had assigned an analyst to work full time in OSR, resulting in closer collaboration between OSR and NSA on the use of SIGINT in OSR's military analysis and production. Finally, Clarke discussed OSR's growing use of computer support and advanced data processing during the previous five years, including the increased use of the QUIKTRAK military forces database and the SCAM military costing database.

Clarke made a separate announcement in June 1972 that the Factory Markings Staff of OSR was being disestablished and that DIA's Joint Factory Markings Center would assume its responsibilities. He also mentioned that DIA's new joint center would include a small unit staffed by OSR. Clarke had included a short section on the activities of the Factory Markings Staff in each previous annual report; he did so his 1972 report as well.

Schlesinger Era

CIA experienced considerable turmoil in 1973 as a result of the abrupt dismissal of DCI Richard Helms in late 1972 and his replacement with James Schlesinger in February 1973. Schlesinger had done a study of the Intelligence Community at President Nixon's request in 1971 while at the Bureau of the Budget, and he came to the Agency with a strong mandate to reduce CIA's budget and personnel. Schlesinger stayed on only until July 1973, however, when he left to become Secretary of Defense. Vernon Walters was acting DCI until William Colby replaced him in September 1973. Colby was Schlesinger's executive director, and the two worked closely together to implement the DCI's proposed changes, most of which focused on cutbacks to the clandestine service. Colby completed many of the reductions after Schlesinger left.

Schlesinger also wanted to strengthen the DS&T. His first step was to transfer NPIC from the DI to the DS&T.[10] He did so to give NPIC better access to advanced exploitation technology. The transfer took place in July 1973, at which time Lundahl retired from CIA. Lundahl was replaced as head of NPIC by John Hicks, who previously had been the chief of the Regional Analysis Division of OSR and was familiar with NPIC's imagery support to military analysis. Thus NPIC's move to the DS&T had little negative impact on OSR, and relations between the two even improved. Next, Schlesinger abolished FMSAC and created the Office of Weapons Intelligence (OWI) in the DS&T, which was tasked to do research on both offensive and defensive weapons systems. This action was completed in September 1973. OWI was headed by David Brandwein, the former head of FMSAC, so its relations with OSR changed little. Furthermore, Clarke had developed a close relationship with Carl Duckett, the DDS&T.

Clarke welcomed the arrival of Schlesinger; he had gotten to know Schlesinger when the new DCI was head of International Programs at the Bureau of the Budget. The two clearly got along well. Clarke said that Schlesinger was fascinated with OSR's military-economic analysis of the Soviet defense budget and was an eager but demanding customer. Clarke believed that the new DCI had an extensive background in strategic matters and had firm ideas about how CIA's support to policymakers could be improved. One of these was to revamp the process for producing military estimates. Schlesinger wanted shorter NIEs designed for an executive reader that summarized essential information and key judgments. The detailed backup data and analysis would be put into an annex.[11]

1973 Annual Report

Clarke's final annual report for FY 1973 was dated July 1973 and written with Schlesinger's departure and Colby's arrival as the new DCI in mind.[12] It was essentially a summary of OSR's activities in support of the Nixon administration beginning in 1969. Clarke began his report with a brief history of OSR's accomplishments for the year. He stated that OSR's four main tasks during 1973 were to provide intelligence to support the formulation of national security policies; draft major portions of national intelligence estimates on military subjects; perform research and analysis on the military programs, capabilities, and defense expenditures of the Soviet Union, China, and other foreign countries; and provide policymakers with current intelligence on foreign military developments and their implications. The policy support efforts pertaining to SALT included both monitoring the SALT I interim accords and preparing for new strategic arms negotiations to be undertaken in November 1972, termed "SALT II." In the MBFR arena, OSR's support efforts increased as the prospects for serious negotiations grew. Talks with the Soviet Union were scheduled to begin in the fall of 1973. OSR also participated in a new series of NSSMs ranging from ones on US policy toward NATO to US strategic military interests in the Pacific.

Clarke then went into some detail on OSR's support to policymakers for SALT. He stated that the intelligence burden continued to increase as President Nixon's second administration got under way. The signing of SALT I in May 1972 had placed a heavy demand on the Intelligence Community to monitor compliance with the accords. OSR took the lead in producing an interagency evaluation of US capabilities to monitor compliance with the interim agreement on offensive weapons, and it contributed to a study OSI led on monitoring the ABM treaty. In addition, OSR's Regional Analysis Division began to produce regular SALT Monitoring Reports on Soviet activities relevant to the accords, including new developments that raised concerns about the potential for future violations. These studies and reports were prepared under the direction of the SALT Monitoring Steering Group that DDCI Walters chaired. Before Helms left his DCI position in early 1973, he had made it clear that CIA's role was to lead the effort to monitor treaty compliance, and that the Verification Panel of the NSC had the responsibility to determine whether any actual treaty violations had occurred.

Clarke then turned his attention to OSR support to policymakers for SALT II, which included separate rounds of talks in Geneva in November 1972 and March 1973. As in SALT I, a CIA intelligence advisory team was sent to support each session. Stoertz headed the first team, and OSR's executive officer, Robert Hewitt, led the second. OSR prepared reports on a variety of issues pertaining to the talks, including the status of Soviet strategic forces and the procedures for destruction of missile launch sites.

The upcoming MBFR talks in October 1973 were to include reductions in US and NATO theater forces in Europe on one side and Soviet and Warsaw Pact forces on the other. As a result, Clarke stated that preparations for the negotiations had taken on a new urgency; OSR represented CIA on an NSC interagency working group that produced a policy paper outlining the US approach. OSR also contributed to a study of US capabilities to monitor reductions in Warsaw Pact forces. President Nixon sent the policy paper to the United States' NATO allies after it was approved by Kissinger. As a result, Clarke added that the issue of Warsaw Pact defense spending became a hot political topic because of its potential impact on NATO defense budgets.

Clarke next mentioned that OSR contributed heavily to two key NSSMs in 1973. NSSM-168 was a comprehensive study of NATO strategy, US programs supporting NATO, and US policy options. OSR prepared an evaluation of Warsaw Pact forces for operations against NATO. It also participated in a lengthy review of papers on NATO strategy, mobilization, and force status. Clarke added that these revealed serious shortcomings in US knowledge about the capabilities of NATO forces.

The other contribution was to NSSM-171 on US strategy for Asia in the aftermath of the Vietnam peace accords. It was the first done since President Nixon's visit to China and the resultant detente that followed. It examined the interplay among the national interests of China, the Soviet Union, and the United States in the region as background for policy decisions on US force deployments. OSR drafted sections on Chinese ground force capabilities and on the military strategy underlying China's defense posture. It also provided a detailed assessment of the North Korean military threat to South Korea. Finally, OSR also contributed to NSSMs on US chemical weapons policy, US nuclear policy, and US naval force missions.

Clarke next addressed the heavy role that OSR played, along with FMSAC and OSI, in the drafting of detailed military estimates on Soviet and Chinese military forces. These included the traditional ones on Soviet strategic offensive and defensive forces as well as NIEs on Soviet military power in distant areas, Soviet forces in Asia and the Sino-Soviet border situation, and Soviet military operations in Eurasia. The other NIEs were on China's strategic attack forces and China's general purpose forces. Clarke then mentioned that future military estimates that OSR drafted would be done under DCI Schlesinger's new guidelines for shorter estimates prepared for busy policymakers.

Clarke provided more detail on OSR's own military research efforts in addition to those done in direct support of US policy. The policy support work helped OSR focus on problems that were likely to be of most future importance to decisionmakers as well as to improve analytic techniques and data processing. Clarke said that OSR was increasingly emphasizing the effectiveness of foreign military forces as well as military doctrine and strategy. He added that the office was also making progress on net assessments of the relative capabilities of opposing military forces. In addition to examining various elements of Soviet strategic forces, such as new ICBMs and SSBNs, OSR was also studying command and control of the Soviet Union's strategic forces.

Clarke stated that research on Chinese and North Korean forces, in contrast to similar research for the Soviet Union, was still in the basic data-gathering phase. This effort was being greatly assisted by new satellite imagery, which for the first time was providing extensive area coverage with higher-resolution imagery adequate for better assessment of various Chinese military programs. Progress was also being made in the joint effort with DIA to assess the size and deployment of China's ground forces. One result was that the accepted estimate of the size of China's ground force was increased from 2.4 to 3.5 million men.

Clarke next addressed the continued challenge to OSR's military-economic research on Soviet defense spending. DIA had first questioned the validity of OSR's methodology in 1972, leading to the decision by DCI Helms and DDI Proctor to establish a Military Economic Advisory Panel of cleared economists from outside the government. DCI Schlesinger appreciated OSR's costing efforts, but he also believed that OSR's estimate that Soviet defense spending was only six or seven percent of total GNP was too low, and he supported the need for an outside review. As a result, Paisley helped to recruit cleared members, and the first meeting of the panel was held in April 1973. It was chaired by Professor Holland Hunter of Haverford College—a widely recognized expert on the Soviet economy—and included several other experts drawn from both the US defense industry and academia. Three more meetings followed before the panel issued its initial report in July 1974.[13]

Clarke then focused on foreign military activities that led to current intelligence reporting by the Regional Analysis Division in 1973, often done in conjunction with FMSAC and OSI. These included the testing of three new Soviet ICBMs, sea trials of the new Soviet D-class SSBN, and the launching of the first Soviet aircraft carrier. Other events included Soviet naval deployments to the Caribbean, Indian Ocean, and Persian Gulf; several failed tests of China's first ICBM; and Egypt's expulsion of Soviet forces and advisers at a time of increased military tensions with Israel. These developments were all reported in CIA's standard current intelligence publications, including the PDB, as well as in several new special updates that Schlesinger had established to go directly to Kissinger and Nixon.

Clarke next provided updates of OSR's efforts to improve intelligence collection and exploitation in conjunction with NPIC and NSA, as well as the progress being made in data-handling and computer applications. Much of the focus of both efforts was on China, which remained a serious analytic challenge because of major gaps in CIA's knowledge of Chinese military programs and capabilities. QUIKTRAC was being expanded to handle military data on both China and the Middle East, SCAM's defense costing system was being improved, and other new databases were being established to handle cost analysis data on Chinese military developments.

As he had done every year, Clarke concluded his 1973 annual report with a summary of OSR's intelligence production, this time over the entire six years of its existence. He noted that the number of OSR's own research publication had risen steadily until 1970 and then began a decline that continued into 1973. He attributed this decline to the increased direct drafting of more detailed military estimates by OSR analysts beginning in late 1970. Clarke noted that the exception to the general trend was an upswing in reports on Chinese and other Asian communist military forces, which he attributed to increased policymakers' demands as well as to improved collection efforts.

Clarke's Departure and Other Changes

President Nixon had announced in May 1973 that Schlesinger would be his next secretary of defense. He replaced Schlesinger as DCI with William ("Bill") Colby. Before Schlesinger left in July, he asked Clarke to be his OSD representative to the MBFR talks scheduled to begin in Vienna that fall. Clarke got Colby's agreement to go for one year, which ultimately became extended to a six-year absence from CIA. He returned in 1979 and was appointed by DCI Turner to replace Robert Bowie as head of the National Foreign Assessment Center (NFAC).

Before Clarke left in September 1973 to move to Vienna, Austria, he made several major changes in OSR's organizational structure. The first was the creation in September 1973 of a Strategic Evaluation Center (SEC).[14] The center's mission was to expand OSR's work on net force assessments and foreign national security policy, with the main focus on the Soviet Union. The idea to do so came from DCI Schlesinger, who wanted to have a focal point in the DI for strategic military analysis that added political, economic, and technical expertise to the mix. A joint DI/DS&T task was created to study the issue, headed by Fritz Ermarth, a former RAND expert on Soviet policy whom Schlesinger brought into CIA. The study recommended that the SEC be created and located in OSR, with Ermarth as its chief. It was initially staffed by analysts from the former Strategic Evaluation Branch of OSR's Programs Analysis Division.

Ermarth stated that Schlesinger was also unhappy with NIEs being done on the Soviet Union, particularly on Soviet military intentions, and that he asked Ermarth to see how they might be improved.[15] The Soviets had begun testing a new series of more advanced ICBMs with potential MIRVed warheads soon after the SALT I treaty was signed, and policymakers were increasingly concerned that Moscow might have been seeking a strategic military advantage through force modernization within treaty limits. The Soviet ICBM force had grown faster than CIA had estimated during the late 1960s; by the time the treaty was signed, the Soviets already had a larger but less sophisticated force than the United States.

In the spring of 1973, Schlesinger commissioned a new special national intelligence estimate to assess Soviet intentions. Robert Gates, who was then serving in the ONE staff, was asked to do a first draft, and Ermarth was tasked to do a tougher rewrite. Released in late September 1973 as SNIE 11-4-73, *Soviet Strategic Programs and Détente: What are They Up To?*, the SNIE portrayed a more aggressive Soviet policy that might seek some strategic advantage but not clear-cut superiority. The services all dissented, seeing the Soviets as seeking a decisive shift in the strategic balance of extended deterrence that would permit them to pursue other global objectives without US interference. This divergence of view was to continue for the next several years.[16]

Clarke clearly designed his second major organizational change to help support him in his new position in Vienna. It went into effect on 1 October 1973 and was announced by Clarke's successor as D/OSR, Henry Knoche.[17] Clarke had briefly created a new Western Forces Division in OSR to focus on both Soviet Bloc and NATO countries, but just before he left, he abolished it and created two new divisions, one for Soviet Strategic Forces and one for Theater Forces (initially named Warsaw Pact-NATO Division). The Soviet Strategic Forces Division was to concentrate on SALT support and provide analysis to NIEs on Soviet strategic offensive and defensive weapons systems as well as naval forces. The Theater Forces Division was to focus on analysis in support of MBFR matters and on NIEs on Warsaw Pact and NATO military issues.

Clarke's departure from OSR to join the MBFR talks in Vienna as the DoD representative happened relatively quickly, but he did all he could to leave the office in good shape for his successor. He handpicked the leadership team for each component of OSR resulting from the reorganization before he left, and he designated many of them as "acting" if they were in new positions. Clarke's decision to leave was not entirely unexpected because he had told several of his senior managers that five or more years in the same position was long enough for any leader, and that it was time for a change.[18] Although Clarke was gone, he was not soon forgotten by all those who had worked for him and by those who provided intelligence support to the MBFR talks in Vienna.

❖ ❖ ❖

Endnotes

1. See NIE 11-8-69, *Soviet Strategic Attack Forces*, 9 September 1969.

2. Details on the interactions of DCI Helms and DDI Smith with ONE and the DI can be found in Knapp, *The Central Intelligence Agency*, 258-264.

3. "OSR Annual Report for Fiscal Year 1971," July 1971, 6.

4. Ibid., 10.

5. "OSR Personnel Directory," 15 April 1971.

6. "OSR Annual Report for Fiscal Year 1971."

7. "OSR Annual Report for Fiscal Year 1972," July 1972.

8. NIE 11-4-72, *Issues and Options for Soviet Military Policy,* 2 March 1972 and NIE 11-12-72, *Soviet Military Research and Development*, 19 September 1972..

9. Firth and Noren, *Soviet Defense Spending*, 46-47.

10. Details on Schlesinger's action as DCI are in Knapp, *The Central Intelligence Agency*, 309-315.

11. Clarke, interview with James Hanrahan, 25 April 2002.

12. "OSR Annual Report for Fiscal Year 1973," July 1973.

13. Firth and Noren, *Soviet Defense Spending*, 46-47.

14. "OSR Organization," 12 September 1973.

15. Ermarth, Fritz, interview with Judy Oliver, 2 December 1999.

16. CIA. NIE-11-4-73, *Soviet Strategic Arms Programs and Détente: What Are They Up To?*, 10 September 1973.

17. "OSR Organization," 21 September 1973.

18. Firth, interviewed by Robert Vickers, 31 December 2016.

❖ ❖ ❖

Chapter Five: 1973–75

Knoche Becomes Director of OSR under DCI Colby

Although Hank Knoche's appointment as director of OSR was unexpected, he had a good reputation as senior staff officer. Knoche had joined the Navy in 1943 and was commissioned as a midshipman a year later. He then studied Chinese at the University of Colorado and became a Navy SIGINT officer before transferring to NSA in 1951, where he remained as a civilian after his discharge. He was recruited by CIA in 1953 and joined OCI as a Chinese military analyst. Knoche had several special assignments in the mid-1950s pertaining to the Suez and Taiwan Straits crises. He served in the front office staffs of both DCIs McCone and Raborn in the early 1960s and was the executive director of NPIC from 1967 to 1969. He also served as the deputy director of OCI from 1970 to 1972 and was the director of the Foreign Broadcast Information Service (FBIS) from March 1972 to September 1973."[1]

Knoche's Team

Knoche inherited a strong core of experienced OSR senior managers and analysts.[2] These included his deputy, John Paisley, and his executive officer, Robert Hewitt, both of whom had served in these positions the previous several years. They also included Ben Rutherford as special assistant for MBFR, T. Stanley Mace as special assistant for SALT, and Randy Payne as special assistant for forces coordination. Paisley retired in mid 1974 and was replaced as deputy by Noel Firth, who had just returned from the National War College. Hewitt also left and was replaced as executive officer by Omego Ware. Clarke had carefully picked the new senior and midlevel managers in OSR resulting from his decision to create the new Soviet Strategic and Theater Forces Divisions just before he left. These senior managers (listed in the paragraph below) served Knoche well over the next two years, particularly because he was absent much of the time doing special tasks for DCI William Colby.[a]

The OSR organizational structure under Knoche in mid-1974 included a number of new division and branch chiefs who were later to hold senior positions in CIA (see chart, OSR 1974, opposite). The new Strategic Evaluation Center (SEC) was headed by Fritz Ermarth, with Fred Hosford as his deputy. Ermarth led the SEC until early 1976, when DCI George Bush selected him to head the newly created Office of Performance Evaluation in the Intelligence Community staff. While there, Ermarth helped organize the A-Team/B-Team effort, which will be discussed later. He stayed there until mid-1977 under President Carter and DCI Turner, when he left to return to RAND. Ermarth returned to Washington a year later to join the NSC staff under Zbigniew Brzezinski and remained there until early 1981. In early 1984, DDI Gates appointed Ermarth to be the NIO for the USSR; after a two-year stint at the NSC as senior director for the Soviet Union and Europe, in early 1988 Ermarth became chairman of the National Intelligence Council, a position he held until 1993.

The new Soviet Strategic Forces Division was headed by John Vogel, with Frank Reynolds as his deputy. Reynolds had been chief of the USSR/Eastern Europe Branch in the Regional Analysis Division in 1971 and before that headed the Aircraft Systems Branch in 1967. He later became head of the new Office of African and Latin American Analysis in 1981 and the Office of Current Production and Analytic Support in 1984. The division had two new branch chiefs: Almon Roth led the new Command Analysis Branch and Morgan Jones led

a. Charlie E. Allen, who had a long and distinguished career in CIA, joined OSR in early 1973 under Bruce Clarke and was appointed the deputy chief of the task force. He was a great admirer of Clarke and regarded the task force experience as a defining moment in his leadership style, for which he was awarded a medal of merit. Charlie Allen interview, 17 July 2009.

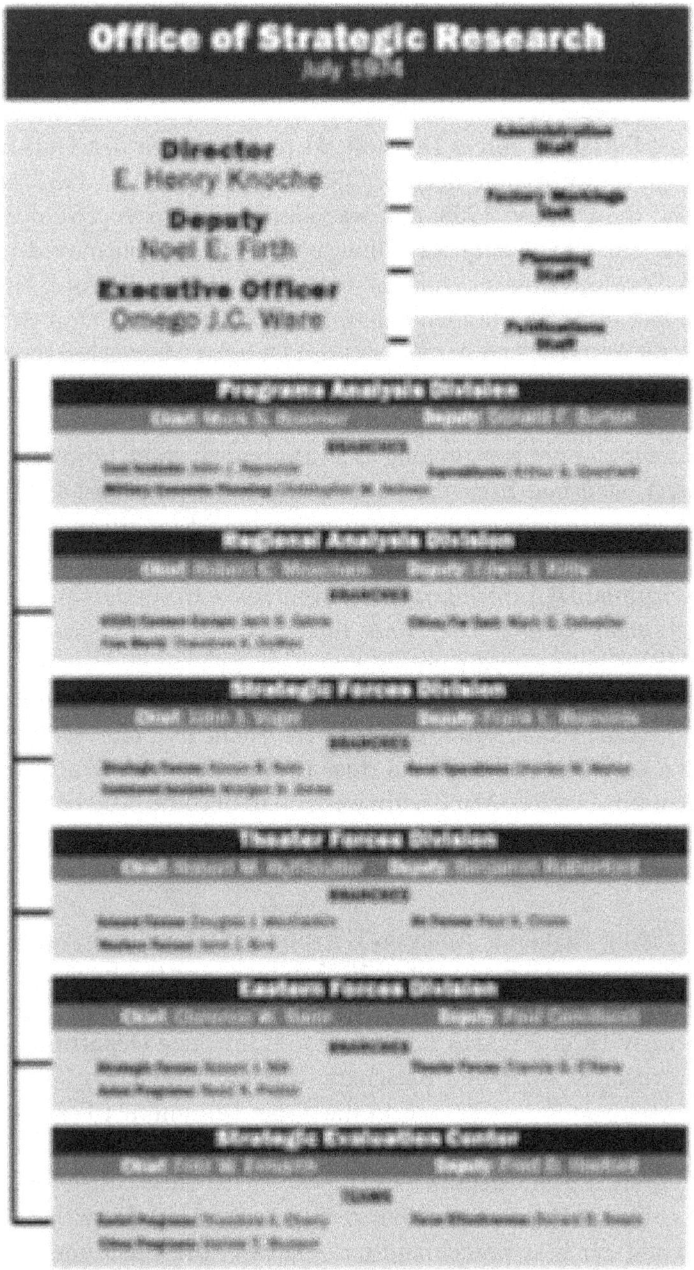
Office of Strategic Research
July 1974
Director
E. Henry Knoche
Deputy
Noel E. Firth
Executive Officer
Omego J.C. Ware
Programs Analysis Division
Regional Analysis Division
Strategic Forces Division
Theater Forces Division
Eastern Forces Division
Strategic Evaluation Center

the Strategic Forces Branch. Charles Walter remained head of the Naval Operations Branch.

The new Theater Forces Division was run by Rae Huffstutler, who had previously been head of the Strategic Defense Branch in the Soviet and East European Forces Division. As mentioned earlier, Huffstutler would go on to become head of OSR in 1979, SOVA in 1981, NPIC in 1984; the DDA in 1988; and was named CIA's executive director in 1992. His first deputy was Omega Ware, who soon moved up to become executive officer and was replaced by Ben Rutherford. The division had three new branch chiefs: John Bird for NATO forces, Paul Cheek for Warsaw Pact Air Forces, and Douglas MacEachin for Warsaw Pact Ground Forces.

MacEachin did not stay on long as a new branch chief, however.[3] Carl Erickson, who had been the head of the Soviet and East European Forces Division before the reorganization, and Rutherford, who had been his senior analyst for general purpose forces, had been selected as the two initial DCI intelligence representatives to support the MBFR delegation in Vienna. They took turns serving as the Washington, DC, MBFR talk's coordinator and rotating to Vienna. In early 1974, MacEachin was asked to replace Erickson in Vienna. After two rotations there, he was designated as the permanent DCI representative in Vienna, where he maintained a close relationship with Bruce Clarke. As mentioned earlier, MacEachin went on to become head of SOVA in 1984, the head of the Arms Control Intelligence Staff in 1989, and the DDI in 1993.

The existing Regional Analysis Division also had new leadership. George Allen had left as chief in 1972 to take over the Imagery Analysis Staff and was replaced by Ray Firehock, who had been his deputy. By early 1974, Firehock had left to join the State Department, and he was replaced by Robert Meacham, who had previously been head of the Strategic Forces Branch in the Asian Communist Forces Division. Meacham inherited Edwin Kilby, who previously had led the Free World Branch, as his deputy. Ted DuMez stayed on as chief of the Free World Branch. The two new branch chiefs were Mark Detweiler of the China and Far East Branch and Jack Gains of the USSR and Eastern Europe Branch.

The Asian Communist Forces Division had been renamed the "Eastern Forces Division" by early 1974, and it also had new leadership and a new Asian Programs Branch. The new division chief was Clarence Baier, who had previously been the deputy chief under Lou Sandine, and the new deputy was Paul Camillucci, who had been head of the previous Theater Forces Branch. The branch chiefs were Robert Will of the Strategic Forces Branch, Frank O'Hara of the Theater Forces Branch, and Reed Probst of the new Asian Programs Branch. O'Hara and Probst were new branch leaders.

Finally, the Programs Analysis Division had new leadership as well. Mark Boerner had replaced Firth as the chief and Don Burton became his deputy. Burton had previously led the Military Economic Planning Branch in the division and was replaced by Chris Holmes. This was Holmes's first OSR management position; he would eventually become the director of the Office of Scientific and Weapons Research (OSWR) in 1994. John Reynolds was the new chief of the Cost Analysis Branch, and Bill Tomlinson was the chief of the new Expenditures Implications Branch.

The Yom Kippur War

Soon after Knoche arrived in OSR, one of the most significant intelligence failures in CIA's history occurred: the surprise Egyptian and Syrian attacks in Israel on 6 October 1973—often referred to as the "October War" or the "Yom Kippur War." Much has been written about the conflict, and how the crisis played out will not be detailed here. Like the Cuban Missile Crisis, however, although CIA did not anticipate the Arab offensive, it redeemed itself with the excellent intelligence support that it provided to help Kissinger arrange a cease-fire and negotiate a settlement. Richard Lehman of OCI set up a Middle East Task Force (METF), which included analysts from OCI, OER, and OSR, to support the Nixon administration's handling of the crisis. The key interagency forum was the Washington Special Action Group (WSAG), which the DCI attended. The METF produced daily reports for WSAG during the next several weeks up until 19 November, when tensions eased.[4] OCI was responsible for the political input, OER the economic, and OSR the military. During the height of the fighting, OSR played a key role in providing intelligence about the combat situation.

A particularly tense period of the conflict occurred on the night of 24 October, when DCI Colby called the CIA Operations Center from the White House because of growing concerns by WSAG about potential Soviet military intervention. The author of this study was then working in OSR's Free World Branch, which covered the Middle East, and happened to be assigned to night shift that evening with an OSR Soviet military analyst. Israeli forces had driven the Egyptians back across the Suez Canal and trapped the Egyptian Third Army, and Moscow had threatened to take military action unless a cease-fire was arranged. The branch then received reports that Soviet airborne forces had been put on alert. After several calls from Colby for updates, Kissinger decided to put US military forces on alert as a signal to Moscow. During the next several days Kissinger worked hard to get a cease-fire declared, and the crisis soon eased. CIA won high praise from both President Nixon and Kissinger for its intelligence support during the conflict.

Colby's Changes

One of Colby's first actions as DCI, even before he was sworn in, was to abolish the Office of National Estimates and replace it with a new team of National Intelligence Officers (NIOs) under George Carver.[5] In doing so, Colby followed the scheme that Helms had used for Vietnam and Schlesinger for the Near East of appointing a senior intelligence expert to be a single focal point on a regional or functional subject of national interest. The new NIOs were to report directly to the DCI on issues of concern to the entire Intelligence Community. They also were to maintain close contacts with their counterparts in the NSC and other government agencies. Finally, rather than draft national intelligence estimates themselves, they were expected to tap the best analytic experts from within the Community and to oversee the coordination process. The first several NIOs were all CIA career officers, but others were drawn from the rest of the Intelligence Community and from academia. The goal was to have about 12–15 NIOs widely regarded for their regional or functional expertise and able to produce intelligence assessments that were directly relevant to policymakers' interests.

From the perspective of OSR, the most important NIO was Howard Stoertz, the first NIO for Strategic Forces. As mentioned earlier, Stoertz had been appointed head of the DDI's Imagery Analysis Service in 1967, and he stayed there until mid-1972, when he was replaced by George Allen from OSR. While at IAS, Stoertz's imagery analysts worked closely with OSR's military analysts to evaluate the imagery from each new satellite mission, and IAS provided valuable intelligence input for most of OSR's military research efforts. After Stoertz was appointed head of the DCI's SALT support group in mid-1972 and began to provide intelligence support to the SALT negotiating teams in Geneva, he continued to work closely with OSR's Soviet military analysts. This close relationship continued when Stoertz became the NIO for Strategic Forces.[6]

In late 1973, Colby also created a new Office of Political Research (OPR) in the DI to complement the functional expertise in OSR and OER. Headed by Ramsey Forbush, who had been the acting director of ONE, its mission was to do in-depth analysis on the internal political affairs and foreign policy issues of those countries of key concern to policymakers. The office would also help draft NIEs and contribute current intelligence items to the new National Intelligence Daily (NID), which Colby created in early 1974. OCI produced the NID in a newspaper format for a high-level audience on a daily basis. President Nixon, Kissinger, and a few other senior officials continued to receive the more sensitive PDB. With the introduction of the NID, the Current Intelligence Bulletin was transformed into the National Intelligence Bulletin (NIB). Although produced by CIA, it included articles from other intelligence agencies and was coordinated throughout the Community.

Also in 1974, Colby completed the process of turning the Operations Center into an all-Agency component with permanent duty officers from each directorate. The DDI still ran the center, but the name was changed from the "OCI Operations Center" to the "CIA Operations Center." To expedite coordination in crisis situations, the center was provided with updated electronic communications facilities that linked it to other agency centers. It was eventually able to provide a secure conferencing capability for intelligence centers throughout the Washington, DC area.

Key Developments in OSR

Within OSR during 1974, two key developments were the first report of the Military-Economic Advisory Panel and the full staffing of the Strategic Evaluation Center. As stated earlier, Helms decided to create the MEAP in 1972 based on a recommendation from DDI Proctor, primarily in response to a complaint from DIA that challenged the validity of CIA's estimates of Soviet military spending. It took two years to staff the panel with cleared nongovernment economic experts and for the panel members to hold enough meetings to complete their initial study. The MEAP remained an active advisory group for the next 20 years, with new expertise coming and going, and it continued to provide an unbiased outside perspective on CIA's military-economic effort.

In its first report, the panel defined its mission as trying to help CIA do a careful evaluation of communist military and economic activity. The report endorsed CIA's analytical approach to costing Soviet defense spending and estimating overall Soviet GNP. But it noted that the separate effort of comparing Soviet defense spending to US spending was a complex task of ruble-to-dollar conversion that created confusion and skepticism among potential users, including defense officials and Congressional budget planners.[a] It concluded that OSR should create a manual to explain the costing process to analysts in other agencies.[7]

About the same time that the MEAP report was issued, Secretary of Defense Schlesinger asked for a CIA paper on the Soviet defense burden. Despite Schlesinger's earlier complaints while DCI that he thought CIA's estimate of Soviet defense spending was too low, the new CIA paper barely raised the defense burden to 6–8 percent of Soviet GNP. DIA

a. The ruble was not a freely traded currency. Its value against the US dollar was artificial, thus making comparisons more difficult.

Director Daniel Graham raised strong objections to the paper when he saw a final draft. He stated that a nonexpert could conclude that the Soviet defense effort was substantially less than that of the United States, primarily because it absorbed an almost equal percentage of GDP in an economy nearly half the size of the US one. In response, Proctor promised to produce a more exhaustive study the following year to explain the Soviet defense burden and the US comparison in more detail. In addition, OSR and DIA created a joint Military Costing Review Board to act as a clearinghouse to resolve conflicting costing procedures between the two agencies.

The CIA study, issued in April 1975, was the most complete analysis done to that point on the burden that Soviet defense spending put on the economy. It concluded that Soviet leaders did not perceive defense costs as a major economic burden and that rising defense costs were unlikely to restrain the Soviets unduly in the future. The paper added that a dollar comparison of US and Soviet defense programs indicated that Soviet expenditures had exceeded those of the United States every year since 1971 and were 20 percent higher in 1974.[8]

Meanwhile, Fritz Ermarth and Fred Hosford worked hard in 1974 to get the SEC up and running. Two key problems were space and personnel. SEC was initially staffed with analysts from the Programs Analysis Division, and some time was needed to recruit additional military systems specialists from other DI offices. Renovating enough space to locate the initial complement of staff in the same location took another year. Meanwhile, recruitment continued so that SEC could reach its full staffing level. The goal was to have three teams within SEC: Soviet Programs, China Programs, and Force Effectiveness Analysis.[9]

Some of the major responsibilities of the center were to do net force assessments of Soviet and Chinese military forces in relation to those of the United States and to develop new intelligence techniques and methodologies to measure force effectiveness. This was a tall order, and the demand for contributions to national estimates and to the SALT and MBFR negotiations took much time and effort. As a result, basic research and the development of new analytic methodologies suffered. Nevertheless, SEC developed a variety of models to enhance its ability to generate quantitative comparisons of US and Soviet strategic forces and to conduct strategic force interaction analysis. The office also continued to improve its capability to conduct theater forces net assessments. These were often done with assistance from cleared government contractors.

By the end of 1974, SEC had nearly completed its first major research paper, "Soviet Commentary on US General Purpose Forces." OSR had been concerned that while the United States was procuring increasingly complex and costly weapons for its ground forces, the Soviets might be following a strategy of buying enough cheaper weapons to equip a much larger ground force that could overwhelm NATO forces by sheer numbers. Research by the Programs Analysis Division found that instead, the Soviets were impressed with advanced US weapons technologies and were shifting to more complex and expensive weapons for their ground forces. The SEC study raised the issue of whether the Soviets were seeking clear military superiority over US and NATO ground forces.

1974 Annual Report

At the end of FY 1974, OSR produced another annual report.[10] Unlike the previous reports issued under Bruce Clarke, the 1974 report was issued by the OSR planning staff with no accompanying distribution notes from D/OSR Knoche. The report was also done in a new format based on the concept of Management by Objectives introduced by DCI Schlesinger and continued by DCI Colby. The system was meant to direct CIA resources to the highest-priority problems, which were set by a list of objectives created by the DCI staff. Each subordinate component would do likewise, showing how it would meet the DCI objectives as well as its own. At the end of each year, the components would measure their accomplishments against the listed objectives.

The 1974 report made clear that the second round of SALT talks and the beginning of MBFR negotiations placed heavy demands on OSR for increased intelligence support to Kissinger and the NSC staff as well as to the negotiating teams. In addition, the introduction of the two new intelligence publications, the NID and the NIB, led to increased demands for current intelligence reporting. This plus the increased volume of information from satellite imagery and crisis reporting, such as on the Arab-Israeli conflict, resulted in an explosion of OSR's current intelligence production. Such items increased by more than 100 percent compared to the previous year. The demands for policy support and current intelligence reporting affected OSR's own research production, which dropped 30 percent compared to FY 1973.

The report provided far less detail on the substantive production of each OSR division as was done in previous annual reports. Instead, it focused on how OSR was meeting each of its 12 objectives, many of which were not directly related to intelligence production. The first objective concerned future OSR contributions to NIEs and SNIEs as well as NSSMs and other NSC memorandums but did not list contributions during FY 1974. OSR projected that it would provide support to at least three NIEs and 10 NSSMs in FY 1975.

Objective two involved an OSR survey of databases pertaining to potential future global crisis areas in FY 1975 to ensure they would meet intelligence support needs. The report stated that OSR had worked with other DI analysts to develop a list of potential crisis areas and with senior NIOs to survey Intelligence Community databases on each area, but progress was slow. Objective three related to selecting techniques for producing net assessments concerning US, Soviet, and Chinese military interactions. The report said that the new SEC was working to accomplish this objective.

Objectives four and five concerned a review of all OSR ADP applications and databases, particularly those pertaining to Soviet, Warsaw Pact, and NATO military-economic activity during 1974 to support the SALT and MBFR talks as well as for intelligence input into future NSSMs and net assessments. The report stated that major progress had been made toward these objectives in FY 1974, both by upgrades to costing data on prices and ruble-dollar exchange rates and as a result of the establishment of the MEAP and the Military Costing Review Board. The report added that the new availability of Soviet military equipment, obtained as a result of the 1973 Arab-Israeli War, had resulted in "hands on" cost exploitation. Some of the ground force weaponry was found to be much more complex, and hence more costly, than was previously estimated. Little progress had been made on costing overall NATO and Warsaw Pact forces, however, because of a paucity of pertinent data.

Objective six dealt with developing more detailed databases on Chinese military forces in FY 1974. This was to be done by taking advantage of greater photographic and SIGINT coverage of China. The report stated that the databases on Chinese ground forces were being expanded. It added that, despite a large volume of information in the strategic and air defense field, little had been done to expand the databases because of a shortage of resources.

Objective seven involved reviewing OSR's intelligence relationships with other Intelligence Community components so all components could better share their common workloads. The report stated that OSR had reviewed its planned intelligence production within CIA and that a joint study done by the DI and DS&T production offices had been forwarded to the two deputy directors. In addition, OSR was working with DIA to compile an accurate order-of-battle of Warsaw Pact forces to support the MBFR negotiations and to develop net force assessments. It was also working with DIA to coordinate procedures for costing the Soviet defense budget.

Objective eight addressed reviewing and improving guidance to intelligence collectors. The report stated that OSR had initiated a new program to brief outgoing military attaches and chiefs of station on collection needs and requirements. It added that particular attention was being paid to providing continuous collection guidance to NPIC and NSA and that a person from each of these components was detailed to OSR full-time to refine requirements and troubleshoot when any problems occurred. OSR was also making extensive preparations for the advent of a new satellite imagery collection system, the KH-11, which had greatly increased capabilities compared to older photographic systems.

Objective nine dealt with completing the full transfer of OSR's joint Factory Markings Center to DIA by passing full administrative control of all personnel to DIA. This was done during 1974.

Objective ten concerned satisfying OSR's personnel requirements during the ensuing year. The report stated that OSR had recruited over 25 military analysts, economists, and military systems specialists during 1974 to meet staffing needs, and that 10 more were in the process of being hired. Nevertheless, the office was still understaffed, and new positions had been authorized for FY 1975.

Objective eleven related to upgrading the performance capabilities of OSR personnel through improved training and additional foreign travel. The report said that all training records for OSR mangers had been reviewed and that future training needs for FY 1975 had been determined. Additional training requirements for division-level managers were also identified and scheduled for the following year. Particular attention was paid to ADP training for analysts. About 35 percent of the analysts had already attended at least one ADP course, and 30 analysts were scheduled for FY 1975.

Finally, extended foreign orientation travel was scheduled for some analysts during 1974. Although short-term foreign trips for OSR analysts were fairly common, these extended TDYs were designed to assist analysts in obtaining information for in-depth research papers on key military topics. The author of this study was fortunate to be one of the analysts to complete such travel in mid-1974, with the result that the author was able to produce the first OSR research paper on the capabilities of a close military ally. The author did so with the knowledge and support of the host military and visited several military bases and production facilities in the process.

Objective twelve addressed providing enhanced equal employment opportunities in OSR for women and minorities. Despite considerable efforts, this proved to be difficult to achieve. Most new analysts whom OSR recruited in its early years had college degrees and had completed their military service obligations as a result of the Vietnam-era draft. Most of the women and minorities applying to fill analytic positions in CIA in the early 1970s were not interested in military analysis and sought positions as political or economic analysts. Nevertheless, OSR hired several women professionals in 1974, the brightest spot in its equal employment opportunity (EEO) efforts. For example, Rae Huffstutler recruited Helen Reed in late 1971 to join OSR's Strategic Defense

Branch in the Soviet and East European Forces Division. Reed eventually became the chief of the Strategic Forces Division in the early 1980s in SOVA and then the head of the Mobile Missile Assessment Center in the DS&T.

The FY 1974 report ended with a review of the key military issues that consumed OSR resources in 1974, the level of analytic production, and a preview of the coming year. The key issues included SALT and MBFR support, the developing Chinese strategic forces, and the military situation along the Sino-Soviet border, which remained tense. New interest had arisen in the military forces and programs in Free-World countries of strategic importance to US security policy. Finally, interest continued in the economic costs of Soviet and Chinese military programs and their potential as future threats to US national security.

The report mentioned that OSR had produced over 2,000 current intelligence items along with 61 basic research and support papers. The current intelligence items included those in the new NIBs and NIDs as well as for new White House Special Reports. The research and support papers included continued SALT monitoring reports and periodic reports for the White House on the status of Soviet strategic forces. In addition, OSR continued to issue preliminary assessments of all satellite missions in collaboration with NPIC.

The look-ahead section was particularly interesting. It stated that OSR was obviously a very busy office and was running short of much-needed money, people, and space. The report added that continued ADP upgrades were much needed but costly, and that this situation was forcing OSR to choose between cheaper quick fixes and more expensive longer-term solutions. The increased demand for current intelligence reporting and policy support was negatively affecting in-depth research and production, and OSR lacked enough manpower to do both. Finally, while OSR was getting more positions, it did not have enough space to accommodate new people.

The FY 1974 report then mentioned three major analytic challenges that OSR was trying to deal with in the coming years. The first was the continued lack of inter-office and inter-directorate research planning. The report stated that while the need for coordinated research planning was widely recognized, progress beyond that had been poor. It added that in part this was because of the heavy demands on all offices to meet policy demands. The report bluntly stated, however, that boundaries among the various offices in the DI and DS&T—including OSR, OER, OCI, OPR, OWI, and OSI—remained stubborn despite strong and sincere efforts to improve coordination. The report concluded that any solution would have to come from the directorate level.

A second challenge was planning for the advent of the new KH-11 satellite system, which was anticipated within the next two years. In fact, the first mission was launched in December 1976. The KH-11—the first electro-optical satellite—took digital imagery that could be immediately transmitted to global ground receiving stations. The older satellites took photographic images that were stored in large film buckets. The buckets were dropped into the ocean when full and then retrieved and flown to special US processing facilities before being delivered to the Intelligence Community for exploitation; a considerable time-lag resulted before that occurred.

The KH-11 satellite was to be put into a sun-synchronous orbit so that images could be taken continuously in daylight and available for exploitation on a 24-hour basis. OSR was acutely aware that when the new system became operational, large volumes of digital imagery would be continuously available in near-real time. As a result, OSR and all other DI offices that used imagery as a key source would need to be prepared to issue intelligence reports quickly. The FY 1974 report recommended that the most affected offices form an inter-directorate senior review group be formed in FY 1975 to begin planning for the new imagery system.

In fact, Bruce Clarke had sent Richard Kerr in 1972 to join a special study group to help the DI and DS&T prepare for the advent of the KH-11. Ray Cline, the former DDI, headed the group, which included Roland Inlow, Clarke's first deputy, who had become the chief of the Committee on Imagery Requirements and Exploitation (COMIREX) in 1969. Once the study was complete, Kerr stayed on as Inlow's deputy at COMIREX.[11]

The final future challenge mentioned in the report was DCI Colby's desire to make greater use of US intelligence analysis to further US policy interests with key foreign allies. The MBFR talks were already requiring much more sharing of US intelligence on the Soviet Union and Warsaw Pact with various NATO countries beyond the traditional close relationship with the United Kingdom and Canada. The report stated that increasing intelligence sharing with other key allies, such as Germany, was a delicate topic. It would require close coordination of the intelligence sharing activities of CIA, DIA, and the State Department to ensure that the intelligence released to various NATO allies was fully cleared.

White House Shakeup

OSR apparently did not produce any more annual reports for the DDI after 1974, but the office remained busy despite considerable turnover in the Nixon administration. Vice President Spiro Agnew had resigned in October 1973 and was replaced by Gerald Ford in December 1973. Vice President Ford began receiving the PDB every day, and by mid-summer 1974, when Nixon's presidency clearly was in trouble, CIA intelligence briefings of Ford were stepped up. Nixon resigned on 9 August 1974, and soon after Ford was sworn in, Nelson Rockefeller was appointed Vice President. Throughout this transition, Kissinger retained his primacy in the national security field as both Secretary of State and National Security Advisor and continued his heavy demand for CIA intelligence input.

In January 1975, Knoche moved up to DCI Colby's staff to help coordinate the CIA response to various congressional requests for information on CIA activities growing out of Seymour Hersh's explosive *New York Times* article of 22 December 1974 on CIA covert operations against antiwar dissidents and student groups. As a result, Noel Firth ran OSR until June 1975, when Colby appointed Knoche as his assistant deputy DCI (ADDCI) for the Intelligence Community.[12] Knoche's tenure as head of OSR had sharply contrasted with Bruce Clarke's. Clarke had been a very hands-on manager who also gave his senior leadership considerable initiative; Knoche was the complete opposite.

Even when Knoche was not busy doing tasks for DCI Colby, he apparently preferred to let OSR run itself.

❖ ❖ ❖

Endnotes

1. E. Henry Knoche, interviewed by R. Cargill Hall, 24 January 2000.
2. "OSR Organization Chart," 1974.
3. Douglas MacEachin, interviewed by Ed Dietel, 13 July 2007.
4. See Emile A. Nakhleh, "The June 1967 and October 1973 Arab Israeli Wars" in *CIA, Directorate of Intelligence*, 203-235 for examples of CIA reporting during the 1973 conflict. Also see Colby, William and Forbath Peter, *Honorable Men: My Life in the CIA*, Simon and Schuster, 1978, 366-367.
5. See Knapp, *The Central Intelligence Agency*, 320-324 for DCI Colby's organizational changes during his tenure.
6. Howard Stoertz, interviewed by James Hanrahan, 8 May 1999.
7. Firth and Noren, *Soviet Defense Spending*, 46-48.
8. Ibid 54-56.
9. "OSR Annual Report for Fiscal Year 1974," July 1974.
10. Ibid.
11. Richard Kerr, interviewed by James Hanrahan, 7 September 1999.
12. Noel Firth, interviewed by James Hanrahan, 13 August 2002.

❖ ❖ ❖

Chapter Six: 1975–76

Lehman as Director of OSR, Bush Becomes DCI

Lehman and His Team

In June 1975, Richard Lehman was selected by DDI Edward Proctor to replace Hank Knoche as D/OSR. Lehman, in turn, was replaced as head of OCI by William Parmenter. Lehman had graduated from Harvard University in 1944, served in the US Army in World War II in the Pacific Theater, and earned a graduate degree at the University of Virginia. He was then recruited by CIA and joined ORE in 1949 to do economic analysis of the Soviet Union. When DCI Walter Bedell Smith abolished ORE in 1950, Lehman moved to the newly created OCI, where he became chief of its Economics Branch in 1951. He remained in OCI for the next 14 years. One of his most significant accomplishments was the creation of the President's Intelligence Checklist, the PDB's predecessor during the Kennedy administration. Lehman also ran the operations center during the Cuban Missile Crisis. He became the deputy chief of OCI in 1966 under Drexel Godfrey, whom he replaced as director in 1970.[1]

Like Knoche before him, Lehman was surprised by his appointment, but having been in the OCI front office for nearly a decade, he was ready for a change. Lehman inherited a strong OSR leadership team that served him well because, like Knoche, he spent much of the next year doing special tasks for Colby. Colby was concerned that Congress would pass new legislation to revamp the Intelligence Community once its investigations were complete. Within weeks of Lehman's arrival in OSR, Colby formed a special group of senior intelligence officers to study how the Community should be organized. It was headed by the deputy comptroller, James Taylor. In addition to Lehman, the group included Les Dirks from the DS&T, George Carver from the NIC, Gail Donnelly from the DA, and William Wells from the DO. The group labored for several months, with Lehman doing much of the drafting, before issuing its study in October 1975. Referred to as the "Taylor Report," the study focused on strengthening the DCI's authorities and recommended a separation of the DCI from CIA. Colby liked the report and passed it to the White House, but it never saw the light of day and was buried in CIA's files. After the study was completed, Colby asked Lehman to remain in the DCI front office to help deal with Congress; Lehman never returned to his OSR office.[2]

In early November 1975, Colby was summoned to the White House by President Ford and asked to resign. This was part of a major shakeup of Ford's national security team, which included Secretary of Defense Schlesinger being replaced by Donald Rumsfeld and Henry Kissinger giving up his national security post to General Brent Scowcroft but remaining on as Secretary of State. Ford had already decided to replace Colby with George H. W. Bush, who at the time was heading the US Liaison Office in China. Colby agreed to remain in office until Bush was confirmed as DCI. Colby then asked Lehman to provide intelligence briefings to Bush until the new DCI was sworn in, which took place on 30 January 1976. After Bush arrived at CIA Headquarters, Lehman was asked to continue in his position as a special assistant to the new DCI.

Firth and His Team

At this point, Lehman decided to designate Noel Firth as acting director of OSR, a position Firth held until November 1976. Firth took over an OSR organization little changed since mid-1974, although several new managers had been appointed at the office, division, and branch chief levels.[3] John Vogel, the former head of the Soviet Strategic Forces Division, had moved up to the front office to replace Omego Ware as the executive officer. Vogel had been replaced as chief of the Strategic Forces Division by Philip Waggener, and Vogel's former deputy, Frank

Reynolds, had moved to the Strategic Evaluation Center as Fritz Ermarth's deputy, replacing Fred Hosford.

Waggener's new deputy for Soviet strategic forces was Charles Walter, the former head of the Naval Operations Branch. Ronald Reimann was Walter's replacement as the new naval branch chief; he joined Morgan Jones, who had stayed on as the head of the Command Operations Branch, and Frank Ruocco, who was the new chief of the Air and Missile Forces Branch. This was Ruocco's first management position; he subsequently became the head of NPIC and later the DDA, both times replacing Rae Huffstutler. The mission of the division remained focused on SALT support, contributions to NSSMs and NIEs, and producing other studies pertaining to Soviet strategic military issues.

Several other new division and branch managers in OSR were designated by early 1976. By then the Theater Forces Division was being run by Ben Rutherford, who replaced Huffstutler in 1976 when Huffstutler left to attend an allied defense school. The renamed Western Forces Branch was headed by Almon Roth, who replaced John Bird; and the Ground Forces Branch was led by Frank O'Hara, who replaced Doug MacEachin. The Air Forces Branch was still under Paul Cheek. The division's mission remained focused on intelligence support to the MBFR talks.

The Eastern Forces Division continued to be headed by Clarence Baier and Paul Camillucci, but it had four new branch chiefs. Sydney Jammes was in charge of the Asian Programs Branch, replacing Reed Probst, who took over the Theater Forces Branch, succeeding Frank O'Hara. Mark Detweiler then headed the Strategic Forces Branch, replacing Robert Will, who ran the new Middle East/South Asia Branch. In September 1974, Knoche had created a Middle East Study Group in the division in response to the increased importance of the region as a potential crisis area in the wake of the 1973 Arab-Israeli War and the growing Soviet military presence in the region. The study group was tasked to do in-depth research on the Middle East military balance; by July 1975, it had been made a full branch.

Robert Meacham and Edwin Kilby continued to head the Regional Analysis Division, and Ted DuMez continued to lead the Free World

Branch. Joan Phelan was then running the USSR/Eastern Europe Branch, replacing Jack Gains, and R. Sams Smith was back as head of the Asian Branch, replacing Mark Detweiler. The division continued to be a heavy producer of current intelligence on military-related issues for various CIA publications.

Finally, the Programs Analysis Division also had new leadership, with Don Burton as the new chief, replacing Mark Boerner, and John Reynolds replacing Burton as the deputy. William King moved up to become the new chief of the Cost Analysis Branch, replacing Reynolds, while Chris Holmes and William Tomlinson remained heads of the Military Economic Planning and Expenditure Implications Branches. The division continued to focus on military-economic intelligence and was working on a major reassessment of Soviet ruble defense spending.

By then SEC had become a division-level unit organized on a task force or project basis. It had three team chiefs: Donald Swain for Force Effectiveness, Ted Cherry for Soviet Programs, and Harlow Munson for China Programs. Under Ermarth, it had evolved more as a RAND-style think tank with a loosely defined mission rather than as a research and production unit. It was tasked to do integrated studies with other CIA organizations and to provide analysis that other intelligence components did not routinely perform. It also provided analytic support on major national policy and national intelligence issues, including national net assessments, and studied new strategies for arms control verification. Finally, it initiated research on new intelligence analytic techniques and methodologies and provided a forum for interaction among the various components of the IC, particularly with DoD.

Soviet Defense Spending Estimates

No sooner had Firth taken over as acting director of OSR when two significant challenges to its intelligence analysis emerged, both of which had lasting political implications. The first pertained to OSR's estimates of Soviet defense spending, and the second covered CIA's analysis of Soviet military intentions. In May 1976, CIA published the classified and unclassified findings of a major OSR-OER reassessment of Soviet defense spending in rubles. It was based on information obtained during the previous year from joint CIA-DIA debriefings of a Soviet emigre with knowledge of the Soviet defense budget as well as on higher OSR estimates of the prices paid by the Soviets for weapons procurement. According to the new estimates, Soviet defense spending had increased from 40-50 billion rubles in 1970 to 55-60 billion rubles in 1975—an increase of almost 75 percent over the previous CIA ruble estimate of the Soviet defense budget for each of those years. Overall, the annual growth rate of Soviet defense spending was then thought to be 4–5 percent per year, in contrast with the previous estimate of 3 percent. Finally, CIA then estimated that the Soviet defense budget was absorbing 11-13 percent of GNP, in contrast with the previously believed 6-7 percent.[4]

The CIA reassessment emphasized that because about 90 percent of the increase in the defense spending estimates resulted from a better understanding of actual ruble prices rather than the discovery of new or larger Soviet military programs, the revision did not affect CIA's appraisal of the size or capabilities of Soviet defense forces. For example, it significantly increased the estimated ruble costs of Soviet naval ship production but not because any new naval programs had been identified. Nor did the higher ruble spending estimates significantly change the dollar valuation costs of Soviet defense programs, which were based on what the US defense industry would spend to produce the Soviet military arms and material, including the costs of research and development and maintenance. The bottom line, however, was that previous CIA ruble–cost assessments of Soviet military programs clearly had been too low; the Soviets were devoting more economic resources to defense spending than CIA had previously estimated.

Appearing before a Senate subcommittee in May 1976, DCI Bush defended the reassessment, stating that he was favorably impressed with the IC's constant reexamination of old judgments based on the constant flow of new information, and that estimates should be revised as appropriate without partisanship or fear of bias. The reaction to the revision in the policy community and in Congress was not nearly as positive, however; the sudden change created deep and lasting skepticism of CIA's military-economic analysis among some policymakers and members of academia.

One of the harshest critics of the CIA reassessment was Gen. Daniel Graham, the director of DIA at the time. He had been critical of the Agency for several years and publicly maintained that only DIA's intervention prevented CIA from dismissing the emigre's information. Chris Holmes, who was chief of OSR's Military Economic Planning Branch at the time, maintains the opposite. He was present when the emigre was brought to Washington for follow-up questioning and interrogation. Holmes said that it was he who dispelled any suspicions raised by DIA about the emigre's credibility.[5]

Noel Firth maintains that a central irony of the incident was that institutional support for CIA's analysis and its acceptance in the policy community became the weakest when the work itself was at its best. One major consequence of the revision was that OSR was able to get a substantial increase in analytic research and computer support to improve its military spending databases. In its second annual report to DDI Proctor in early 1976, the MEAP urged that OSR put more resources into upgrading its work on Soviet research and development, and it continued to support the quality and value of OSR's Soviet defense spending analysis.[6]

A Team/B Team

The second major challenge to CIA's intelligence analysis of the Soviet Union occurred in mid-1976 with the so-called A-Team/B-Team exercise. By this time, several major changes had taken place in CIA's senior leadership.[7] In July 1976, DCI George Bush selected Hank Knoche to replace General Vernon Walters as DDCI. Earlier that year, Sayre Stevens had been appointed the DDI, replacing Ed Proctor, and Les Dirks had succeeded Carl Duckett as DDS&T. In addition, Richard Lehman had replaced George Carver as deputy to the DCI for national intelligence. This left Noel Firth as acting director of OSR under a new CIA senior leadership team. Meanwhile, Fritz Ermarth had left the SEC in

May 1976 to join the DCI's Intelligence Community Staff and had selected Don Brown from the DS&T to succeed him.

The genesis of the new challenge to CIA's Soviet analysis was the dissatisfaction of certain hardline members of the President's Foreign Intelligence Advisory Board (PFIAB) with NIEs done in the mid-1970s on the Soviet strategic threat. President Eisenhower originally created the Board in 1956 to review the foreign intelligence activities of US government agencies, particularly those of CIA. President Kennedy disbanded and then revived PFIAB in the early 1960s, and in 1972 President Nixon tasked the Board to do annual assessments of CIA's Soviet strategic forces estimates. The PFIAB challenge to the Soviet strategic NIEs began in 1974 when its chairman, Admiral George Anderson, objected to a key judgment in the previous year's estimate that the Soviets were not likely to be able to negate the United States' strategic nuclear deterrent capability during the next 10 years.[8] Anderson was concerned that the threat was more immediate and that CIA was underestimating the continued growth of Soviet strategic attack forces, much as it had done in the mid-to-late 1960s.

The real issue behind the PFIAB challenge to the Soviet strategic estimates was that of Soviet military intentions. The 1973 Soviet strategic forces NIE raised the question of whether the Soviets were seeking some form of strategic nuclear superiority but concluded that the leadership had not decided whether to accept strategic parity or seek clear-cut superiority. The military services all dissented, judging that the Soviets foresaw a decisive shift of the strategic balance in their favor. Nevertheless, the overall judgment of the NIE remained that despite expected improvements in Soviet forces, the Soviets were extremely unlikely to conclude that they could launch a preemptive nuclear strike that would prevent a devastating US retaliation.[9]

Meanwhile, an ad hoc subcommittee of PFIAB members had formed to advocate an experiment in competitive analysis with vigorous pro-and-con advocacy on key strategic issues; parallel but separate estimates were being done by groups inside and outside the IC. The PFIAB members agreed that the issues that needed to be addressed included Soviet ICBM accuracy, Soviet low-level air defense, and Soviet strategic intentions. They persuaded Anderson to send a letter to President

Ford in August 1975 advocating the experiment in competitive analysis, stating that the 1974 NIE was seriously misleading in a number of key judgments and in projecting a sense of complacency unsupported by the facts. The letter was then passed on to DCI Colby.

Colby did not oppose more rigorous pro-and-con argumentation, but he was not receptive to the idea of parallel estimates. George Carver, Colby's deputy director for national intelligence, and Howard Stoertz, the NIO for strategic programs, had carried on an extended dialogue with several members of PFIAB over the 1974 NIE. They found that a conservative faction of PFIAB—including Anderson, Robert Galvin, John Foster, and Edward Teller—believed that the Soviet strategic forces NIEs continued to seriously underestimate the Soviet threat. These members believed that despite the SALT I and Anti-Ballistic Missile (ABM) treaties, significant improvements in Soviet strategic attack and defense capabilities put each leg of the US strategic triad at risk. In particular, the improved accuracy of MIRVed Soviet ICBM missiles made US Minuteman missile silos more vulnerable; advances in Soviet air defenses posed a threat to a US B-52 bomber attack; and improved Soviet anti-submarine warfare (ASW) capabilities put US ballistic missile submarines at increased risk. In short, the members of PFIAB thought that the US policy of detente was working in favor of the Soviet Union, which was seeking a decisive strategic advantage.

Colby responded to the PFIAB letter in November 1975 by stating that the members' concerns about the Soviet strategic threat would be addressed in the 1975 Soviet strategic forces estimate, which was about to be released. However, the conservative PFIAB members were not satisfied with the 1975 NIE. By April 1976, after reviewing the key judgments of all Soviet strategic forces estimates published during the previous ten years, PFIAB again requested that new DCI George H. W. Bush approve an experiment in competitive analysis. Although Carver and Stoertz remained opposed to the idea, Bush agreed in May 1976 to conduct the experiment.[10]

The plan was that NIO Stoertz and the IC would work to draft the regular 1976 Soviet strategic forces estimate, NIE 11-3/8-76, by late 1976. Meanwhile, three B Teams would be formed to examine each of the major concerns expressed by PFIAB the previous year. One would examine Soviet ICBM accuracy, a second would look at Soviet low-level air defense, and a third would address the overarching problem of Soviet strategic intentions. The issue of the Soviet ASW threat would not be examined because of the sensitivity of the data. PFIAB would select the various B-Team members from a group of outside experts with skeptical views of Soviet capabilities and intentions. They would be cleared for the same intelligence used in the official estimate, and after they studied the data, they would met with A-Team members drawn from the IC in November 1976 to exchange views on each issue. Finally, the A and B teams for each issue would brief PFIAB, and then the three B Teams would draft an alternative estimate.

OSR and other CIA military and technical analysts from OWI and OSI played a key role in the A-Team/B-Team exercise. Former deputy director of OSR John Paisley was called out of retirement to manage the B Team process and ensure that the members got all the intelligence they required. Various OSR analysts from the Soviet Strategic and Theater Forces Divisions helped to draft the NIE, and they participated in the exchanges with B-Team members on the Soviet air defense and ICBM accuracy issues. Two team leaders in SEC, Donald Swain and Ted Cherry, worked with the B Team on the issue of Soviet strategic intentions and objectives.

The outcome of the exercise varied from issue to issue. Few differences arose in the A Team and B Team views on Soviet low-level air defenses. The IC had just completed a comprehensive review of Soviet air defenses, which concluded that because of technical difficulties, the Soviets would be unable to counter a large-scale, low-level US bomber attack. The B Team responded that the NIE draft did not adequately express unresolved uncertainties and that the Soviets might have believed that they could prevent most US bombers from reaching high-value targets. The differences between the two teams on Soviet ICBM accuracy were more pronounced. The B Team's estimate assumed that Soviet technical developments were on par with US technology. The A Team rejected this assumption as not consistent with the available evidence; the two teams agreed to disagree.

The exchange by both teams on the issue of Soviet strategic intentions and objectives was by far the most contentious and the one that subsequently got the most public attention and had the most lasting political impact. The A-Team members were working-level analysts, not senior managers. Stoertz later lamented that they were focused on a more narrow definition of Soviet strategic intentions based primarily on their analysis of Soviet strategic force growth and capabilities as well as economic factors and constraints, rather than on broader Soviet global political goals and objectives. He added that senior CIA political analysts were not included on the A Team and were absent from the discussions.[11] This was largely because CIA political analysts were tasked to draft the NIEs on broader Soviet strategic intentions, and they worked under the NIO for the USSR and Eastern Europe rather than for Stoertz. Furthermore, the IC's A Team included analysts from the military services and DIA who disagreed with CIA's analysis of Soviet strategic intentions. They took dissenting views and expressed their belief that the Soviets had the attainable objective of achieving the capability to wage a nuclear war and emerge with reserves sufficient to dominate the postwar period.

In contrast, the B Team on Soviet strategic objectives was stacked with well-known hardline experts on Soviet strategic military and political affairs, led by Harvard political historian Richard Pipes. Pipes's team included several vocal critics of CIA's military analysis, including Daniel Graham. The team had a well-defined political agenda of attacking past CIA estimates that had underestimated the growth of Soviet strategic forces, and the team members took a unified view that Soviet strategic posture and capabilities were far more threatening than the CIA estimates indicated. They also charged that the draft 1976 NIE omitted evidence of an undeviating Soviet commitment to achieving global hegemony. Finally, they suggested that CIA's Soviet strategic estimates downplayed the military threat because of a longstanding rivalry between the civilian analysts at CIA, who controlled the language, and the military intelligence analysts, who were forced to take dissents. The team even implied that CIA analysts were subject to political pressures to minimize the Soviet strategic threat because of the implications for detente.

The A and B Teams made their presentations to PFIAB in December 1976, and the B Teams released their final reports. Richard Lehman, who oversaw the final presentations to PFIAB in his role as deputy

DCI for national intelligence officers, met with PFIAB to express his disappointment with the B-Team report on Soviet strategic objectives.[12] Sidney Graybeal, who had replaced Noel Firth as head of OSR in November 1976, labeled the report "high in stridency and low in specific guidance." OSR's view was that the B Team report was a political polemic on Soviet intentions that ignored economic constraints and had no hard evidence to support it.[13]

Meanwhile, Stoertz and the IC continued the normal drafting and coordination process of NIE 11-3/8-76. According to OSR analysts who participated in the exercise, CIA judgments were not greatly influenced by the B-Teams' alternative views, which they largely ignored. Nevertheless, the estimate was a particularly contentious one, primarily because of strong disagreements between CIA and the State Department on the one hand and DIA and the military services on the other over Soviet strategic intentions and capabilities, with the latter generally taking more pessimistic positions.

In fact, stories of the competitive analysis experiment began to leak to the press even before the final B-Team reports were issued. According to the press leaks, the result of the B-Team efforts was to make the NIE more ominous. As a result, when DCI Bush issued the final version of NIE 11-3/8-76, *Soviet Forces for Intercontinental Conflict Through the Mid-1980s*, on 21 December 1976, he attached a cover memorandum to assure recipients that the B-Team input and outside pressure had not been allowed to subvert the integrity of the estimative process. Bush added that the judgments were the best that could be made on the basis of analysis of the available evidence.[14]

The key judgments on Soviet objectives and expectations concluded that the Soviets did not believe that they would have the capability within the coming 10 years to conduct an intercontinental attack while preventing a devastating US response. But they stated that the Soviets were striving to achieve strategic capabilities that would leave them in a better position than the United States if war occurred, and that Soviet leaders might hope that their future capabilities would give them more latitude for pursuit of their foreign policy objectives while discouraging the threat of US military force in response. This was largely the CIA view, and while it went beyond previous CIA judgments of Soviet strategic intentions, it nevertheless drew vigorous dissent from both the State Department and the military services. State argued that Soviet leaders did not entertain, for the foreseeable future, the reasonable objective of achieving a "war-winning" or "war-survival" posture. DIA and the military services all took an opposite point of view, expressing their belief that the Soviets regarded as attainable an objective of waging a nuclear war with the capability to emerge in a dominate position.

Before Bush left office in January 1977, he released another estimate that specifically addressed Soviet intentions, NIE 11-4-77, *Soviet Strategic Objectives.*[15] Again, Bush attached a cover memorandum, explaining that the estimate was a result of the wide range of views within the IC on the issue of Soviet objectives for their strategic forces expressed in NIE 11-3/8-76. Bush added that there was little hard evidence available to resolve the questions raised by this issue, and that as a result, this estimate was designed to help the recipients understand the different opinions, not resolve them.

For the first time, the key judgments were in the form of questions, not conclusions. The estimate summarized the conflicting judgments as hinging on whether the Soviets saw themselves as winning the Cold War or whether they still saw a situation of overall strategic parity and nuclear deterrence. The NIE stated that two key factors could influence either view in the future: the state of the Soviet economy and the ongoing strategic conflict with China. The positions of individual intelligences agencies were not identified in the estimate, but the pessimists viewed the overall trend as favoring the Soviets gaining decisive strategic superiority and overall global dominance. The optimists saw the Soviets as not having a reasonable expectation of gaining war-winning strategic superiority over the United States within the ensuing decade or of achieving a decisive shift to their advantage in the global struggle.

The B-Team Outcome

The longer-term impact of the A-Team/B-Team exercise was both political and analytical. On the political side, the early leaking to the press of the B Team's alternative view raised concerns in Congress that B

Team had influenced the NIE to take a dire tone, despite DCI Bush's cover memo. The staff of the Senate Select Committee on Intelligence (SSCI) did an investigation that concluded that the estimative process had been damaged and that serious questions had been raised in the public and official mind about its integrity. The staff recommended that an impartial board examine the whole experiment. The final SSCI report, issued in early 1978, was highly condemnatory of the B-Team report and largely sided with CIA.

On the other hand, the B-Team report on Soviet objectives was welcomed by those opposed to US detente policy, including conservative political officials and academics from both political parties. The report contributed to the late 1976 formation of the bipartisan Committee on the Present Danger (CPD), which believed that the US needed to increase defense spending and end arms control efforts in order to confront the growing Soviet strategic threat. Its founders included several B Team members, and it would eventually include both future President Ronald Reagan and future DCI William Casey. The CPD would continue to challenge the administration's policy toward the Soviet Union under President Jimmy Carter and gain considerable influence under President Ronald Reagan.

On the analytic side, President Ford was a lame duck by this time, and no further action was taken as a result of the exercise. The intended final step—a review of the competing A-Team and B-Team reports by an outside panel and recommendations to improve the estimative process—was not done, and the competitive analysis experiment was never repeated. Nevertheless, the strong challenge by outside critics to CIA's analysis of the Soviet strategic issue was one of the factors that contributed to further modifications in the estimative process. These included better documentation of key findings, more attention to alternative scenarios and greater use of cleared outside experts.

One of the ironies of the A-Team/B-Team exercise is that at the same time that the IC began to take a more ominous view of Soviet strategic objectives and capabilities, Soviet leaders were beginning to cut back on the rate of growth in defense spending, although this did not become apparent until the early 1980s. As a result, NIEs in this period and later generally erred on the side of overstating the Soviet military threat. In fact, from 1974 through 1986, every year's NIE 11-3/8 overestimated the rate of Soviet strategic force modernization. One result of the A-Team/B-Team exercise could have been a tendency by OSR to err on the high side of its Soviet strategic force projections, although never to the extent of those done by the military services. The State Department was often the lone dissenter on the low side, leaving CIA in the middle.

In retrospect, virtually all the B Team's dire projections of potential future Soviet strategic capabilities in the team's report and those taken in dissents by various military services to the 11-3/8 NIEs were wrong by a wide margin. These included the range of the Backfire bomber, the accuracy of the newer Soviet ICBMs, the deployment of a mobile ABM system, and Soviet ASW developments. Furthermore, the Soviets never deployed the SS-16 mobile ICBM system and never upgraded the SS-20 mobile IRBM system to ICBMs, despite the B Team's assertions to the contrary.[16] Finally, while the B Team suggested that a crucial military confrontation with the Soviet Union could take place within the ensuing decade, by the mid-1980s Mikhail Gorbachev had come to power in the Soviet Union and was urging radical disarmament and other measures to end the Cold War.[17]

Endnotes

1. Richard Lehman, interviewed by Richard Kovar, 29 February 1998.

2. Ibid.

3. OSR Organization and Missions, March 1976.

4. The new 1976 Soviet defense spending controversy is discussed in detail in Firth and Noren, *Soviet Defense Spending*, 59-66.

5. Christopher Holmes, interview with Ed Dietel, 3 June 2009.

6. Firth and Noren, *Soviet Defense Spending*, 68.

7. Knapp, *The Central Intelligence Agency*, 333-366 discusses actions by DCI Bush.

8. NIE 11-3/8-74, *Soviet Forces for Intercontinental Conflict Through 1985*, 14 November 1974.

9. CIA. NIE 11-8-73, *Soviet Forces for Intercontinental Attack*, 25 January 1974.

10. The A Team-B Team episode is covered in depth in Garthoff, "Estimating Soviet Military Intentions and Capabilities" 159-163 in Haines and Leggett, *Watching the Bear* and in

Knapp, *The Central Intelligence Agency*, 363-364. Relevant NIEs can be found in Steury, Intentions and Capabilities, 335-465.

11. Stoertz, interview by Hanrahan, 8 May 1998.

12. Lehman, interview by Kovar, 29 February 1998.

13. Memorandum For: Deputy Director for Intelligence, Subject: "OSR Comments on the Comparative Analysis Experiment on Soviet Strategic Objectives," 4 February 1977.

14. Steury, *Intentions and Capabilities*, 339-364.

15. Ibid, 391-395.

16. Garthoff, "Estimating Soviet Strategic Military Intentions and Capabilities" 166.

17. Ibid, 161-162.

❖ ❖ ❖

Chapter Seven: 1976–79

Sidney Graybeal as D/OSR and Admiral Turner as DCI

The appointment of Sayre Stevens as the new DDI in June 1976 by DCI George Bush came as a surprise because Stevens had been the associate deputy director of the DS&T the previous two years under Carl Duckett and had no previous experience in the DI. Instead, the DDS&T job was given to Les Dirks, who had previously headed the Office of Development and Engineering in the DS&T and had worked with Lehman on the Taylor report for DCI Colby in late 1975. Nevertheless, Stevens did have a strong analytic background as an expert on Soviet defensive missiles, and he had played a key role in providing intelligence support for the ABM Treaty. Stevens also had turned the Office of Research and Development, which he headed from 1972 to 1974, into an organization that provided direct support to both the DI and DO.[1]

Stevens wanted to concentrate all CIA analytic production in the DI. He strongly believed that OSI and OWI belonged in the DI because of the in-depth research and analysis they did in support of national security, and he wanted to transfer them out of the DS&T. Dirks fought the transfers, but Hank Knoche, who was appointed the DDCI in April 1976, supported Stevens. Accordingly, OSI and OWI were moved into the DI in November 1976. In exchange, however, Knoche transferred the Foreign Broadcast Information Service (FBIS) from the DDI to the DS&T at the same time. Knoche believed that the DS&T could better provide much-needed technical collection support to FBIS.[2]

Stevens made several additional changes in the DI's organizational structure in December 1976. The most significant was the abolition of both OCI and OPR. In their place, Stevens created a new Office of Regional and Political Analysis (OPRA) organized into geographic divisions to do in-depth political research and production. At the same time, he created a small Current Reporting Group to take over OCI's former current reporting role. Stevens also created a new Center for Policy Support of high-level officials whose mission—along with the NIOs—was to maintain close contacts with policymakers to ensure they received relevant and timely intelligence support.

Graybeal Becomes D/OSR

Stevens also worked hard to bring new analytic expertise into the DI from outside the Intelligence Community. As a result, he decided to appoint Sidney Graybeal as the new director of OSR in November 1976 to replace Noel Firth, who had been acting director since February 1976. Firth was subsequently appointed by Knoche as the first director of the newly created Office of Imagery Analysis (OIA) in January 1977. OIA was formed from the former Imagery Analysis Service, which previously had been headed by Howard Stoertz and George Allen, to provide more extensive imagery support to CIA. At the time, OIA was co-located with NPIC in the Washington Navy Yard; thus Firth rejoined former OSR senior manager John Hicks, who had been running NPIC since mid-1973. Firth ran OIA until 1980, when he returned to work again for Bruce Clarke as a senior member of the NFAC staff.

Graybeal was a strong choice to head OSR because of his considerable expertise as a Soviet space-and-missile analyst and his long career as an arms control negotiator. He had been a B-29 bomber pilot during World War II and had flown 32 combat missions over Japan, for which he received the Distinguished Flying Cross. Graybeal joined CIA in 1950 as a missile analyst in OSI; by the time of the 1962 Cuban Missile Crisis, he was chief of the Missile and Space Division in OSI. He and Art Lundahl of NPIC ended up giving the first briefing to President Kennedy and his national security executive community staff about the confirmed presence of Soviet medium-range ballistic missiles (MRBMs) in Cuba. In 1964, Graybeal went to the State Department to work in the Arms Control and Disarmament Agency (ACDA), where he got involved in the negotiations for the SALT I talks and the ABM treaty. Soon after the treaties were signed, he was appointed the first commissioner of the Standing Consultative Commission, which was set up to try to resolve any problems that arose regarding treaty monitoring and verification. After serving there from 1973 to late 1976, DCI Bush asked Graybeal to return to CIA to take over OSR.[3]

Graybeal arrived in OSR shortly after the 1976 presidential elections, and it soon became clear that President-elect Jimmy Carter was going to appoint a new DCI. This took some time, however, and after Bush resigned in late November 1976, Knoche remained on as acting director until the arrival of Stansfield Turner in early March 1977. Knoche then reverted to his role of DDCI, where he remained until August 1977. He was replaced first by John Blake as acting DDCI and then by Frank Carlucci in February 1978. Meanwhile, Turner brought in Dr. Robert Bowie from Harvard University in April 1977 to replace Richard Lehman as his deputy to the DCI for national intelligence, and Lehman became Bowie's deputy. Sayre Stevens remained in place as the DDI.[4]

Turner's Agenda

Turner wanted to greatly expand DCI authority over the IC, but it took him some time to accomplish only a small part of what he intended. By the fall of 1977, Turner got White House approval to create three senior managers for the Intelligence Community: one for analysis, one for collection, and one for resources. The first to be selected was Bowie for community analysis. In October 1977 Bowie was given the title of director, National Foreign Assessment Center (NFAC), which included both the NIOs and the DI. Stevens remained in place as Bowie's deputy director and associate deputy director for intelligence (ADDI), and Lehman became an associate director for substantive support. Turner subsequently brought in two other community managers from the outside for collection and resources. While all this was going on,

OSR continued to perform all its normal intelligence tasks, including providing intelligence support to policymakers and to the SALT II and MBFR negotiations, producing analytic research products and current intelligence reports, and drafting NIEs.

Graybeal's Reorganization

In April 1977, Graybeal announced another reorganization of OSR (see 1977 OSR wiring diagram on page 146).[5] By this time, Philip Waggener had replaced Firth as Graybeal's deputy. The major change was an expansion of OSR's Soviet military-economic costing efforts, partially as a result of the 1976 upward revision of ruble defense spending estimates and the requirement for more analytic resources. The former Programs Analysis Division, still under Donald Burton, was expanded and renamed the Military-Economic Analysis Center. The new center had two broad functional areas with a deputy chief for each, one for cost analysis, headed by John Reynolds, and one for programs analysis, led by Donald Swain. The cost analysis area had a Defense Industries Branch under William King and a Manpower and Operations Branch under Alan Smith, each estimating the defense expenditures of the Soviet Union. The Programs Analysis area had a Comparative Analysis Branch, led by Turner Odell, to compare US and NATO defense activities with those of the Soviet Union and Warsaw Pact and an Economic Implications Branch under Sydney Jammes to examine the economic resource considerations affecting defense planning and budgets in the Soviet Bloc. An Analytical Support Group headed by Paul Welsh managed the SCAM computer program.

Chris Holmes remembers that Stevens pushed hard for more interdisciplinary research projects in the DI and asked Holmes to lead a joint research project on Soviet military research and development. By this time, both OSI and OWI had been transferred into the DI. At first, Holmes tried to work with OSI, but he made little progress. Meanwhile, in early 1977, Rae Huffstutler returned from abroad, and Stevens asked him to take the position of DD/OWI under Evans Hineman. Huffstutler took the job and remained Hineman's deputy until early 1979. Holmes said he made very little progress on his project un-

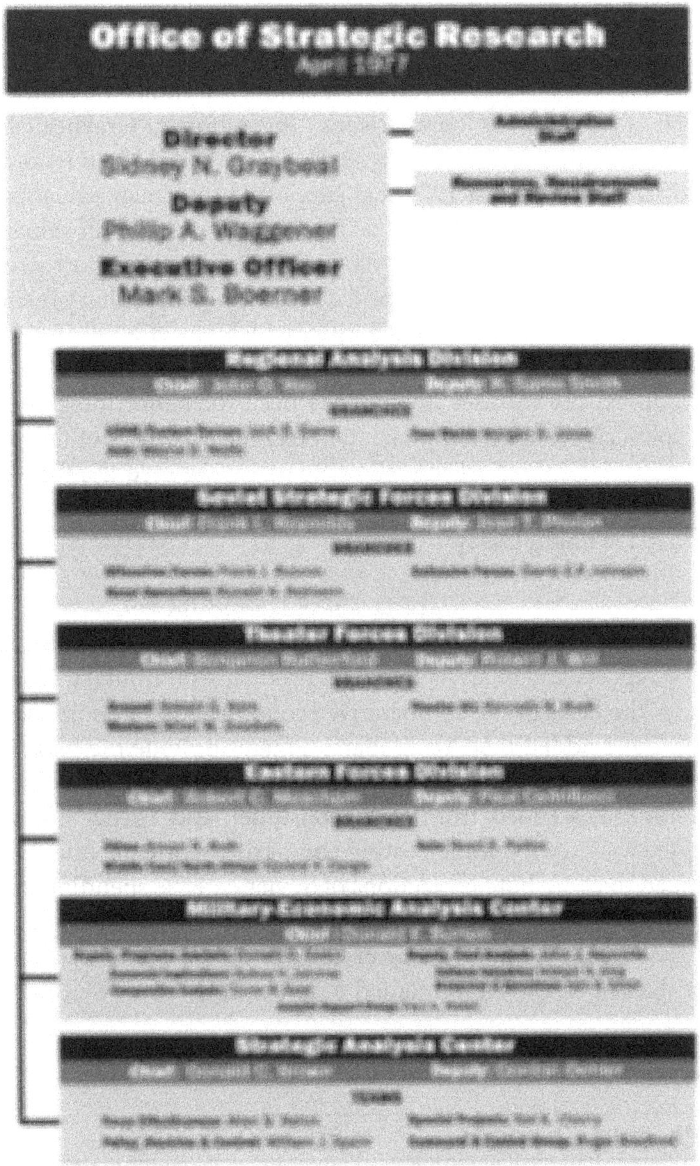
Office of Strategic Research
April 1977
Director
Sidney N. Graybeal
Deputy
Philip A. Waggener
Executive Officer
Mark S. Boerner
Regional Analysis Division
Soviet Strategic Forces Division
Theater Forces Division
Eastern Forces Division
Military-Economic Analysis Center
Strategic Analysis Center

til OSR formed an alliance with OWI to do joint projects, and together the two offices were able to do some useful work.[6]

Meanwhile, Turner had begun to question the utility of OSR's dollar-ruble defense costs comparisons. In response, Graybeal asked MEAP to examine the issue. As a result, a joint CIA/MEAP report was sent to Turner in August 1977 that supported the dollar valuations of Soviet defense programs as well as the estimates of overall valuations of Soviet defense expenditures. At the same time, the report stressed the need for better research on the true cost of Soviet military research, development, testing, and engineering, which was a large and growing share of both US and Soviet total defense outlays. The report went on to address the broader issue of the need for better integration of CIA's political, economic, military, and technical analysis of the Soviet Union. The MEAP report the following year suggested the formation of an office of Soviet studies, an idea that was not achieved until 1981 under DCI William Casey.[7]

President Carter's Secretary of Defense, Harold Brown, also weighed in on the issue. In a 1977 memorandum to Turner, Brown declared that the reports and analysis that CIA produced on military economics were "the basis of the comparative economic analysis employed by Defense" and added that "the dollar estimates provide the best single aggregated measure of US and Soviet defense efforts." This was strong praise for OSR's efforts from a key consumer, and Turner no longer questioned the utility of the costing comparisons. Meanwhile, MEAC continued to contribute projections of Soviet defense spending for the strategic forces NIEs as well as in support of annual DoD budget planning. Nevertheless, the accuracy of CIA's estimates and projections of Soviet defense spending remained a contentious issue well into the next decade.[8]

Leadership Changes

Graybeal's 1977 reorganization resulted in only minor changes in other OSR components, although several leadership changes took place, primarily as a result of transfers, training, and reassignments. The SEC, which Fritz Ermarth and Frank Reynolds headed in early 1976, was now run by Donald Brown, who had previously been in the DS&T, and it included other technical analysts from OSI. The deputy, Gordon Oehler, was also from the DS&T. The center still had three teams, but it altered its scope to focus heavily on the Soviet Union after its China Programs team was abolished. It had a Force Effectiveness Analysis Team led by Allan Rehm, a Policy and Doctrine Team under William Spahr, and a Special Projects Team headed by Ted Cherry. The Policy and Doctrine Team included a Command-and-Control group headed by Roger Bradford from OSI. Bradford had previously worked closely with OSR on Soviet naval issues. The SEC's role remained that of a think tank responsible for providing broad-scale analysis in support of US national security policy formulation. It was expected to produce integrated studies that drew heavily on inputs from other OSR divisions and DI offices and did basic analysis of Soviet command and control.

By then OSR's Soviet Strategic Forces Division was headed by Frank Reynolds, who had moved over from the SEC, and his deputy was Joan Phelan. The division still had three branches, but the former Command Analysis and Air and Missile Branches were abolished and replaced with separate Offensive and Defensive Forces Branches along with the Naval Operations Branch. The division remained the focal point within OSR for SALT support.

SALT Support

Support for the SALT negotiations in Geneva remained a significant responsibility for OSR under Graybeal. The 1972 Interim Agreement limiting Soviet and US strategic offensive forces expired in 1977 but remained in force on a de facto basis thereafter. Meanwhile, a preliminary agreement had been signed in Vladivostok in 1974 that set forth the outlines of a SALT II treaty, but negotiations continued to drag on while both parties continued strategic force modernization. The talks were aimed at limiting the total number of strategic nuclear delivery vehicles, including land-based ICBMs, submarine-launched ballistic missiles (SLBMs), and heavy bombers to 2,400 for each side, along with a limit of 1,320 MIRVed missiles. In addition, the Soviets sought to limit the number of US long-range cruise missiles while the US negotiators sought to reduce the number of Soviet TU-22 bombers. Discussions were also ongoing about the means of treaty verification, limits on new offensive weapon systems, and a ban on improved ICBM launchers.

During the 1973–77 period, Howard Stoertz wore two hats: he was the chief of the CIA SALT Support Team and the NIO for Strategic Programs. Stoertz was replaced as the head of the SALT support team in July 1977 by John Whitman, who remained in that position for the duration of the talks. Stoertz gave considerable credit to both OSR and OWI for their ongoing analytic support to the negotiations. This often required a constant stream of cable traffic and secure telephone calls in response to queries from the negotiators. In addition, CIA analysts from OSR and other offices rotated to Geneva as members of a four-person intelligence support team to assist first Stoertz and then Whitman.[9]

Soviet Military Estimates

Meanwhile, OSR continued to assist Stoertz in his NIO role by producing NIEs on Soviet strategic forces and objectives. The production of these Soviet military estimates between early 1977 and late 1978 placed a heavy burden on OSR's analytic resources during Graybeal's tenure as director. Frank Ruocco, who became deputy chief of the Strategic Forces Division, recalls working 60-hour weeks for months on end to support both Stoertz and the SALT II negotiations. During this period, first Frank Reynolds and then Mark Boerner replaced Vogel as division chief, and Frank Ruocco moved up to become Boerner's deputy.[10]

The task for OSR of producing Soviet military estimates during this period became more challenging because the new NFAC arrangement tended to slow down the production process. According to Lehman, Bowie took a long time reviewing draft estimates; except for military estimates on the Soviet Bloc, the number of NIEs produced began to drop.[11] Unlike DCI Bush, Turner began to take an increasingly

1977 Moscow Parade.

hands-on approach in the substantive process for Soviet military estimates, probably for several reasons. First, he was determined to be seen as a strong DCI in all three areas of Community management: collection, analysis, and resources. He was also only the second senior military officer to head CIA since the pre-Dulles era, and he had a strong background as a naval force commander and a keen interest in military intelligence. Finally, the potential Soviet military threat to US strategic interests and the desire to negotiate new SALT and MBFR treaties were major policy concerns of the new administration, and Turner wanted to please President Carter.

The first Soviet military estimate done under Turner's watch was NIE 11-3/8-77, *Soviet Capabilities for Strategic Nuclear Conflict Through the Late 1980s*, which was not issued until February 1978. Like its immediate predecessors, it was a fairly massive work, produced in two volumes that ran to over 150 pages combined, and it contained major contributions from OSR, OWI, and OSI. The NIE stated that under SALT, the expansion phase of Soviet strategic forces appeared to be over and that the Soviet military was focused on modernization and technological improvement. It noted that the growth rate of the Soviet economy was likely to decline over the next decade, making choices on the allocation of scare resources more difficult. Nevertheless, it forecast that a decline in the growth of Soviet defense spending was unlikely. The estimate did not contain the serious divergent views that characterized previous NIE 11-3/8s about whether the Soviets intended to go beyond nuclear deterrence and achieve strategic superiority under SALT. Rather, it stated that it was less clear that the Soviet political leadership believed that strategic force improvement would lead to a Soviet war-winning posture. It had no footnotes on this issue, although there were others on such previous controversies as the range of the TU-22 bomber, Soviet low-altitude air defense capabilities, ABM developments, and the extent of the Soviet civil defense program. Perhaps in deference to Turner, the Navy did not dissent on Soviet ASW capabilities.

A major innovation that Turner introduced into the 1977 strategic forces estimate for the first time was a limited net assessment of the capabilities of either side to withstand a hypothetical ICBM counterforce attack. The calculations assumed that the strategic forces of each side were constrained by SALT and that the first strike attacks were either by surprise with no warning or preemptive attacks under alert conditions. The calculations were made in terms of which residual ICBMs, SLBMs, and bombers would survive for either side. The idea of even a limited net assessment of a Soviet-US nuclear conflict drew a sharp divergent footnote from DIA and all three military services. They viewed such an assessment as incomplete and falling short of providing any insights into Soviet perceptions, and they objected to its inclusion in the estimate.

The next strategic estimate was on Soviet intentions—NIE 11-4-78, *Soviet Goals and Expectations in the Global Power Arena*, issued in May 1978. It described Soviet leaders as generally viewing the global situation in favorable terms based on the expansion of Soviet military and political influence in the Third World. Despite the expected continued growth in Soviet global influence over the next decade, the estimate noted that the Soviet economy continued to have problems and that its growth had lagged to the point where military spending already exceeded economic growth. The estimate concluded by noting that the aging leadership under Brezhnev was facing a looming succession crisis. This was the first Soviet strategic estimate that raised the issue of future leadership changes and potential economic constraints on Soviet defense spending. Nevertheless, the State Department took a strong footnote to the estimate, believing that it presented too positive a view of Soviet perceptions of their own military power and understated their political and economic problems.

DCI Turner played an even greater substantive role in the next Soviet strategic forces estimate, NIE 11-3/8-78, *Soviet Capabilities for Strategic Nuclear Conflict Through the late 1980s*, issued in January 1979. It was an even more massive work than the previous forces estimate, totaling over 300 pages in two volumes and included a separate annex. Again, it was done with significant analytic input from OSR, including both MEAC and the Soviet Strategic Forces Division. Turner included a transmittal letter noting that then recent evidence indicated that Soviet strategic advances were greater than previously anticipated. The scope note listed four related Soviet strategic estimates that were produced in the same time frame: the previously mentioned NIE 11-4-78; NIE-11-6-78, *Soviet Strategic Forces for Peripheral Attack*; NIE 11-14-79, *Warsaw Pact Forces Opposite NATO*; and NIE 11-10-79, *Soviet Military Capabilities to Project Power in Distant Areas.*[12]

The 1978 NIE delivered a stronger message about advances in Soviet strategic force capabilities than the 1977 version. The overall key judgment was that up until the mid-1980s, Soviet strategic force capabilities would improve relative to those of the West. The only major dissent was again by DIA and the military services to Turner's continued inclusion of comparisons of the residual Soviet and US strategic forces after counterforce ICBM attacks by either side. In response, Turner as DCI stated his own view that such comparisons, along with DoD's own simulations of a nuclear exchange between US and Soviet forces, had merits for the purpose of informing national decisionmakers about trends in the relative capabilities of both forces.

MBFR Support

The Theater Forces Division remained busy as well under Ben Rutherford's leadership in 1977 and 1978. The division was the CIA focal point for intelligence support to the US MBFR delegation in Vienna, which still included both Bruce Clarke as the DoD representative and Doug MacEachin as head of the intelligence support staff. Clarke left

Soviet T-72 tank.

in late 1978 to work for Secretary of Defense Harold Brown as his special assistant for arms control, and MacEachin returned at the same time to become Rutherford's deputy. The MBFR talks were making little progress at the time, primarily because the Soviets refused to release accurate force data on Warsaw Pact forces in support of mutual troop reductions. The US side knew that the Soviet numbers were inaccurate, primarily because of Warsaw Pact force information provided covertly by a Polish military officer, Colonel Ryszard Kuklinski.[13] Meanwhile, the Soviets had begun to deploy SS-20 mobile IRBMs and Tu-22 bombers within range of NATO forces in Western Europe, thereby increasing their nuclear strike capabilities.

In support of the MBFR negotiations, OSR issued two research papers: The Balance of Forces in Central Europe in August 1977 and *The Balance of Nuclear Forces in Central Europe* in January 1978. Then OSR contributed to NIE 4-1-78, W*arsaw Pact Concepts and Capabilities for Going to War in Europe: Implications For Warning Of War*, issued in April 1978. It was not a controversial estimate; its first key judgment was that the Soviet Union and Warsaw Pact were highly unlikely to deliberately attack member countries of NATO under then present circumstances.

In January 1979, CIA published the first comprehensive estimate of Warsaw Pact forces opposite NATO since 1975. Done at the expressed

Soviet Victor III-class submarine.

request of policymakers for a reference document, NIE 11-14-79, *Warsaw Pact Forces Opposite NATO,* was a massive work of over 250 pages in two volumes, and it had significant input from Theater Forces Division. The scope note listed the previously mentioned Soviet military NIEs as well as three related Interagency Intelligence Memorandums (IIMs) on Soviet chemical weapons use, Warsaw Pact manpower assessments, and intelligence denial activities. The key judgments stated that Soviet policy was to maintain forces capable of successfully fighting either a conventional or nuclear war in Europe by keeping a clear numerical advantage over NATO in important military assets. As a result, the Soviets were modernizing their weapons and equipment and increasing the size of their theater nuclear arsenal. The estimate had no major dissents, although some differences arose over nearly two dozen specific issues of weapons use and capabilities, with DIA and the military services generally taking a worst-case view and CIA and State a more moderate alternative. Some of the issues, such as Soviet force readiness and anti-submarine–warfare strategy, were more important than others and therefore received more attention.

A key issue in the NIE that had caught DCI Turner's personal interest was that of Soviet capabilities to interdict NATO sea lines of communication (SLOCs) during a major conflict. The Naval Operations Branch of the Soviet Strategic Forces Division, which was headed by John Bird, had completed a study titled *The Role of Interdiction at Sea in Soviet Naval Strategy* in early 1978 that provoked the concern of the NIO for conventional forces, Admiral John Ekelund, and the US Navy. As a result, OSR spent considerable time and effort responding to Turner's questions and comments on the topic, including producing a memorandum done in preparation for the DCI's meeting with the secretary of the navy. A final assessment of the issue, *The Soviet Attack Submarine Force and Western Sea Lines of Communication*, was completed in April 1979 and included Turner's own views on the subject. The bottom line, which appeared in NIE 11-14-79, was that DIA and the Navy continued to believe that CIA was underestimating Soviet capabilities to interdict Western SLOCs during a NATO conflict.

New Focus on the Middle East

OSR's Eastern Forces Division was also very active during the 1977–78 period. Robert Meacham had been chosen to lead the division in early 1976, replacing Clarence Baier. When Meacham retired in early 1978, Robert Will became the new division chief with Mark Detweiler as his deputy. Graybeal's April 1977 reorganization had reduced the division from four to three branches. The China Forces Branch was formed by combining the former Theater and Strategic Branches and led by Almon Roth. The Asian Forces Branch focused on the Koreas and was headed by James Bohrer. The new Middle East/North Africa Branch was run by Gerald Dargis, who had taken over the Middle East Branch from Robert Will in early 1976 and remained chief after the reorganization. The branch, which focused on the Arab-Israeli military balance, was designed to give more analytic resources to the Middle East region because of continued policymaker concerns about the potential for another Arab-Israeli conflict.

The Carter administration assigned a high priority to trying to broker a peace agreement between Israel and Egypt to reduce military tension in the Sinai. By early September 1978, President Carter had arranged secret talks at Camp David between President Anwar Sadat of Egypt and Prime Minister Menachem Begin of Israel. The resulting Camp David Accords eventually led to the signing of an Egyptian-Israeli

Peace Treaty on 26 March 1979 in which Israel agreed to withdraw all military forces from the Sinai and return the territory to Egypt. It was perhaps Carter's major foreign policy achievement, and both Sadat and Begin were awarded Nobel Peace prizes in recognition of their contributions.

In August 1976, CIA had issued its first major assessment of the Arab-Israeli military balance since the 1973 conflict, and in August 1977, under Turner's watch, it produced a massive update. While NIE 35/36-1-76: *Middle East Military Balance (1976–1981)* was about 85 pages long in a single volume, its successor was over 250 pages in two volumes. Both were done with major contributions from OSR's Middle East Branch. The key judgments of both estimates were that Israel had increased its margin of military superiority of its Arab adversaries since the October 1973 war and would have a decisive advantage in the event of hostilities for at least the next five years. The estimates further stated that the most likely Soviet option in the event of a conflict would be a swift resupply of the Soviet Union's Arab clients and that a war would almost certainly be too short for the Soviets to introduce decisive military forces. The primary reasons for Israel's military advantage over the combined Arab forces were qualitative rather than quantitative, especially leadership, training, and manpower.

OSR's China and Asian Branches

OSR's China and Asian Branches in the Eastern Forces Division were not as active as the Middle East Branch during this period, primarily because their military-related issues did not have the same high policymaker priority as those in the Middle East. The China Branch had contributed heavily to NIE 13-76, *PRC Defense Policy and Armed Forces*, issued in November 1976 just as Graybeal arrived in OSR. In sharp contrast to the Soviet military estimates, it was less than 70 pages long and only projected about five years ahead. It was one of only three military estimates that CIA did on China in the 1970s and superseded ones issued in 1972 and 1974. The scope note stated that in contrast to the Soviet Union, both the quantity and quality of intelligence available on China were seriously deficient. The main key judgment of the estimate was that Peking considers the United States to be less of a direct military threat than the Soviet Union, and that China would seek to avoid a nuclear conflict with either adversary. It concluded that modernization of the armed forces would continue to be slow and uneven.

Later on, the Asian Branch contributed heavily to SNIE 14.2-1-79, North Korean Military Capabilities and Intentions, issued in May 1979. This estimate updated a similar one done in 1975, but it was notably shorter than the Soviet or Chinese military estimates prepared in the same time frame, most likely because of a paucity of hard data on North Korean force size and strength. The North Koreans made heavy use of underground facilities to reduce the vulnerability of their forces, complicating collection and analysis. The key judgments stated that as a result of the continued growth and modernization of North Korea's armed forces during the preceding decade, its military options had increased and it could attack the South with little warning. The warning issue of a surprise North Korean attack was a major IC concern for the next several decades and remains so today.

Like the Theater Forces Division in OSR during Graybeal's tenure, the Regional Analysis Division experienced no organizational changes, only leadership ones. By April 1977, John Yeo had taken over from Meacham, and R. Sams Smith was his deputy. The division continued to have Asian, Free World, and USSR/EE Branches led by Wayne Wolfe, Morgan Jones, and Jack Gains respectively. Its mission remained current intelligence reporting and short-term analysis of military developments worldwide. New analysts were often assigned to the division to learn tradecraft, and turnover tended to be heavy once they gained experience and moved on to research assignments.

In late 1978, Graybeal suddenly decided to retire. His deputy, Philip Waggener, was taken by surprise and did not know why Graybeal had made the decision. Those in OSR who worked closely with Graybeal found him to be bright, personable, and very interested in the work the office was doing. He also appeared to get along well with Stevens and his peers. Perhaps Graybeal knew that Sayre Stevens planned to retire in early 1979, and he decided to leave also. Both left CIA in early January 1979 and subsequently went to work for private industry contractors. By this time, Graybeal had spent over 30 years in the federal government, including his military service. In January 1980, he received the President's Award for Distinguished Federal Service, the highest honor a civilian can receive from the US government. In 1994, he was appointed to the Policy Board of the Department of Defense.

One of the analytic legacies of both Stevens and Graybeal was the greatly improved interaction among OSR, OSI, and OWI that resulted from their efforts. Gordon Oehler, an OWI analyst who served as the deputy chief of the Strategic Evaluation Center, subsequently became the deputy chief of the Strategic Forces Division in 1981 and later the director of the Office of Scientific and Weapons Research (OSWR) in 1984. Chris Holmes, who did joint projects with OSI and OWI while in SEC, went on to become director of OSWR in 1994. Roger Bradford, a senior scientific analyst in OSI who did a rotation as a branch chief in SEC from 1978 to 1980, stated that he learned much about Soviet command-and-control capabilities while working in OSR.[14]

In an interview that Graybeal gave to public radio in early 1998, he was asked what role intelligence had played in the Cold War. He responded that in his view, good intelligence was a critical aspect of the Cold War because it allowed the United States to maintain strategic stability. He added that without intelligence, policymakers would not have known Soviet intentions and capabilities. He said that intelligence was key to verification of the ABM and SALT I agreements. Graybeal's bottom line was that not only was military intelligence important, but so was political and economic intelligence, and that without them, a nuclear conflict with the Soviet Union would have been more likely.[15]

❖ ❖ ❖

Endnotes

1. Sayre Stevens, interviewed by James Hanrahan, 13 May 1999.

2. Knapp, *The Central Intelligence Agency*, 364-366, discusses changes in the DI under DDI Stevens.

3. *Washington Post*, "Arms Control Negotiator Sidney Graybeal Dies at 73," 22 March 1988.

4. Details on Turner's tenure as DCI are derived from two main sources. The first is from Chapter Eight in *CIA, Directors of Central Intelligence as Leaders of the Intelligence Community*, CSI, 2007, available at www.cia.gov. The second source is Turner, Stansfield, *Secrecy and Democracy: The CIA in Transition*, 237-251.

5. OSR Organization and Directory, April 1977.

6. Holmes, interviewed by Ed Dietel, 3 June 2009.

7. Firth and Noren, Soviet Defense Spending, 69.

8. Ibid., 145.

9. Stoertz, interviewed by Hanrahan, 8 May 1998.

10. Frank Ruocco, interviewed by Darb Drewyer, 9 May 2006.

11. Lehman, interviewed by Kovar, 29 February 1998.

12. NIE 11-6-78, *Soviet Strategic Forces for Peripheral Attack*, 12 September 1978; NIE 11-14-79, Warsaw Pact Forces Opposite NATO, 31 January 1979; NIE 11-10-79, Soviet Military Capabilities to Project Power in Distant Areas, February 1979.

13. MacEachin, interviewed by Dietel, 13 July 2007.

14. Roger Bradford, interviewed by Robert Vickers, 22 January 2016.

15. Sidney Graybeal, interviewed by George Washington University for Episode 21, "Spies," 29 January 1998.

❖ ❖ ❖

Chapter Eight: 1979–81

Huffstutler as D/OSR and the End of Turner's Tenure

Rae Huffstutler's appointment as D/OSR in January 1979 marked the beginning of a three-year period of strong leadership of the office by someone who had risen up through its ranks under Bruce Clarke. Huffstutler was familiar with both Soviet strategic and theater forces, and his stint as Evans Hineman's deputy in OWI had given him considerable technical expertise. Huffstutler said he was ready and eager to take over OSR's leadership.[1] Philip Waggener remained as his deputy when he arrived, and Joan Phelan moved up to become the executive officer. By this time, OSR was one of the largest offices in NFAC.

Clarke Becomes D/NFAC

Meanwhile, NFAC underwent considerable change during the final two years of Turner's leadership. The most significant was the return of Bruce Clarke to senior management in CIA. After leaving the MBFR talks in Vienna in September 1978, Clarke had served brief stints in senior positions with Secretary of Defense Brown and Secretary of Energy Schlesinger. He then returned to CIA at Bowie's request in early 1979 to become executive secretary of the NFAC Production Board. In August 1979, Turner was persuaded by Carlucci and Lehman, who was then the NIO for Warning, to replace Bowie as the head of NFAC. Turner asked Clarke if he was willing to take the job. Clarke was more than happy to take over as D/NFAC. He had gotten to know Turner years before when he was D/OSR and Turner headed the systems analysis division in the Navy, and the two got along well.[2]

When Clarke became D/NFAC, his former senior manager, John Hicks, was in place as his deputy. Hicks had replaced Sayre Stevens as ADDI in January 1979 when Stevens retired. Soon after Clarke took over, he made several major changes. In October 1979, he selected Hineman, who was still the head of OWI at the time, to replace Hicks as his deputy. Then he selected Richard Kerr to replace Douglas Mulholland as head of the Office of Current Operations, which had been formed in December 1978 by combining the Current Reporting Group with CIA's Operations Center. Kerr had joined OSR at its creation and had left OSR in 1972 with Clarke's support to head a special study group under COMIREX to prepare for the advent of digital imagery collection satellites. In 1974, Kerr became the deputy of COMIREX under Roland Inlow and then in 1976 became the executive officer of the Intelligence Community Staff. DCI Bush had reorganized the IC Staff in early 1976 under V. Adm. Daniel Murphy, with John McMahon as his deputy. Kerr worked under McMahon for two years and then moved to ORPA in 1978 after Turner appointed McMahon the DDO.[3]

Clarke's next major move came in December 1979 when, with Turner's approval, he created the National Intelligence Council (NIC)—a US government "think tank" staffed by national intelligence officers and their deputies. Lehman, who was the NIO for warning at the time, had suggested the move, and Clarke named Lehman as the NIC's first chairman. Thus for the first time since 1973, when Colby abolished the Office of National Estimates, all NIOs were in a single unit with its own chairman. Finally, in January 1980, Clarke merged OSI and OWI into the Office of Scientific and Weapons Research (OSWR), with Wayne Boring as its director. Boring had become head of OWI when Hineman became Clarke's deputy. Hineman initially opposed the change but agreed when Clarke insisted on having a single technical and weapons analysis office in NFAC.

Huffstutler as D/OSR

Huffstutler was then in the happy position of working under two of his former office directors and mentors, Clarke and Hineman. He was also working closely with former D/OSR Lehman and with Kerr, who had been a fellow OSR branch chief when Clarke was still its director. Like Clarke and Firth before him, Huffstutler strongly advocated military training and rotational assignments to improve the expertise and career opportunities of promising OSR analysts. Thus OSR analysts and managers continued to be sent to various military service schools and courses for more advanced training as well as being assigned to military-related rotational positions that gave them a broader perspective of the intelligence and policy communities.

Huffstutler soon made several leadership changes in OSR in early 1979, mostly because of training, rotations, and retirements.[4] Phil Waggener had decided to retire as OSR's deputy director in early 1979, and Huffstutler replaced him with Frank Reynolds, who had returned from the National Intelligence Tasking Office. In May 1979, Huffstutler made Frank Ruocco head of the Soviet Strategic Forces Division in place of Mark Boerner, who had retired. At the same time, Huffstutler sent Douglas MacEachin to be director of the Strategic Warning Staff at the National Military Command Center in the Pentagon, and he put Ted DuMez in MacEachin's place as deputy chief of the Theater Forces Division.

Perhaps the most interesting leadership change that Huffstutler made during his tenure as D/OSR was to bring in Robert Gates as head of the Strategic Evaluation Center in place of Donald Brown. Gates had decided to leave the NSC in late 1979 after serving under National Security Advisor Zbigniew Brzezinski since May 1977. Huffstutler had a high regard for Gates and offered him the job, which Gates quickly accepted. It was Gates's first senior managerial position in CIA, and he badly wanted it. As fate would have it, Gates's stay in OSR would be short. Turner was having problems interacting with Brzezinski, and he asked Gates to become his executive assistant. Gates was reluctant to leave OSR, but Turner insisted, and Gates took the job.[5] Huffstutler quickly replaced Gates with MacEachin, whom he brought back from the Pentagon.

Carter Administration Crises

The Carter administration experienced considerable turmoil, crisis, and disappointment in its last two years, and CIA would play a major intelligence role in several key issues. Most of the concerns were related to what was seen as increased Soviet aggressiveness and influence in the Third World. The year 1979 began with the overthrow of the Shah of Iran in January, followed quickly by the return of Ayatollah Khomeini and the establishment of a radical Islamic regime. The Iranian situation turned from bad to worse in November 1979 when radical extremists seized the US embassy and held several dozen Americans hostage. A rescue attempt by the US military failed in April 1980, and the hostages were not released until 20 January 1981, the day of President Reagan's inauguration. The bottom line was that the United States lost a valuable strategic ally in the Middle East along with key intelligence collection facilities along the Soviet border.[6]

Meanwhile, the Carter administration had to deal with increased Soviet and Cuban influence in Latin American, Africa, and the Far East. The Soviets continued to provide military arms to Cuba, including Mig-23 fighter aircraft, and they were supporting new Cuban allies in the region. These included Maurice Bishop, who seized power in Grenada in March 1979, and the Sandinistas, who overthrew President Anastacio Somoza in Nicaragua in July 1979. The Soviets had already been supporting Cuban military intervention in Africa, especially in Angola and Ethiopia, and had gained Muammar Qaddafi's Libya as another military client state in the region. Moscow gained another military ally in March 1979 when Vietnam gave it naval access to Cam Rahn Bay and permitted the construction of a major SIGINT collection facility there. This installation was paralleled worldwide only by the Soviet SIGINT facility at Lourdes in Cuba, the largest outside the Soviet Union.[7]

Soviet TU-95 long-range reconnaissance aircraft.

CIA took note of these developments in 1979 by producing two major Soviet military estimates, both done with heavy analytic input from OSR. The first was the previously mentioned NIE 11-10-79, *Soviet Military Capabilities to Project Power and Influence in Distant Areas*, issued in February 1979. It was a detailed review of the Soviets' efforts to expand and strengthen their power and influence in the Third World since the mid-1950s through military aid and arms sales, support of insurgent movements, and the use of friendly military forces—at the time, Cuban ground forces in Ethiopia and Angola. The estimate also examined Soviet capabilities to intervene in various global conflicts through the use of air, air defense, and naval forces. The NIE considered Afghanistan as the one Third World country where the Soviets might intervene with ground forces, but the IC concluded that they were unlikely to do so. The estimate included detailed annexes on notable Soviet military actions in the Third World since 1954, Soviet aid to insurgent movements, major Soviet airlifts and capabilities, and the effect that Soviet military assistance had on the balance of regional forces. The IC's bottom line was that Soviet leaders continued to view the Third World as fertile ground for the expansion of Soviet political, military, and economic influence but that Soviet leaders had no illusions about the difficulties of achieving their objectives.

The second estimate was NIE 11/85-79, *The Soviet Cuban Military Relationship*, issued in December 1979. It took a detailed look at the growing Soviet effort to upgrade Cuba's military forces since 1975 and the corresponding increased Cuban willingness and capability to conduct military operations in the Third World. The IC judged that both sides benefited from the close ties. Cuba got critical economic and military support. The Soviet Union got an effective military addition to its own efforts to expand its global power and influence, as well as the use of Cuba for its own military purposes. These included the SIGINT facility at Lourdes and the use of Cuban ports and airfields for periodic deployments of Soviet air and naval forces. The Lourdes site intercepted US domestic and international satellite communications as well as tactical and strategic US military communications. Soviet TU-95 long-range reconnaissance aircraft (see photo on page 164) staged in Cuba to monitor US naval operations along the east coast for up to four weeks, and Soviet naval surface combatants and submarines also made periodic ports visits, sometimes lasting several months. The estimate concluded that the close military relationship was likely to continue to grow at least over the next several years.

SALT II Hopes

Despite these regional setbacks, the Carter administration continued to pin its hopes on achieving a SALT II agreement with the Soviet Union, particularly because the MBFR talks were not making any progress. At a summit held with the British, French, and West German leaders in January 1979, Carter agreed to deploy new US intermediate range ballistic and cruise missiles in Western Europe to counter the continued Soviet deployment of SS-20 missiles and TU-22 bomber aircraft. In contrast, the SALT II negotiations were moving ahead despite significant CIA concerns about treaty monitoring, and agreement was reached on a draft treaty in May 1979. This set the stage for a SALT II summit and signing ceremony in Vienna on 18 June 1979 by Secretary Brezhnev and President Carter.[8]

The SALT II Treaty set a limit of 2,250 nuclear weapons delivery vehicles for each side by the end of 1981, including ICBMs, SLBMs, and heavy bombers, and it prohibited the development of new ICBMs with significantly improved capabilities. It also set a limit of 1,350 MIRVed missile launchers deployed by either side and prohibited the construction of new land-based ICBM launch facilities. The Soviets were permitted to keep a specific number of SS-18 heavy ICBMs; they secretly agreed with the United States to limit the number of TU-22

Soviet SS-20 IRBM.

bombers produced each year and to limit their range to preclude intercontinental attacks. The United States was allowed to continue development of the Trident SLBM and Tomahawk cruise missile programs. Finally, the treaty's terms were to remain in effect through 1985 if not rejected by either party.

Turner and Gates both have stated that CIA intelligence support was vital to achieving the final agreement. Gates mentions that CIA provided a great deal of intelligence support to the President in preparation for the summit. Turner took a close personal interest in the subject of treaty monitoring and verification because it was a sensitive political issue vital to treaty ratification. As a result, in June 1979 CIA completed a massive detailed study of US intelligence capabilities to monitor Soviet compliance with the SALT II Treaty with significant inputs from OSR, OWI, and OSI. Turner made himself an expert on the topic on treaty-monitoring strengths and weaknesses, and he gave great credit to the enormous skill of CIA analysts to piece together many small fragments of information in support of treaty verification. As a result, he was able to convince the administration that the Intelligence Community had enough confidence in its technical collection capabilities to monitor Soviet compliance with the treaty to support ratification.[9]

Because the Soviets refused to allow on-site inspections for treaty monitoring, the IC needed to rely on its technical collection capabilities to monitor treaty compliance. Two key elements of technical collection were satellite imagery and electronic intercepts, especially of missile telemetry. Telemetry is the signals that test-missiles send back to the ground that provide measurements of performance; the data can indicate a great deal about a missile's capabilities. US intelligence was able to collect the telemetry during Soviet ICBM flight-testing, and the treaty stipulated that each side not interfere with the other's "technical means of verification." The Soviets, however, had been increasingly encrypting these signals, and Turner insisted that the Soviets provide access to encoded telemetry signals to assist treaty verification. Moscow reluctantly agreed, but the issue was further complicated by the loss of US ground collection stations as a result of the Iranian revolution. The solution was an agreement to transfer the collection-monitoring sites to China—a major intelligence bonus resulting from President Carter's earlier restoration of full diplomatic relations with China in December 1978.[10]

Unfortunately, what was supposed to be a crowning arms control achievement of the Carter administration—SALT II—never got ratified by Congress. Two things intervened that prevented Senate ratification. The first was the discovery of a Soviet military unit in Cuba. The second was the Soviet invasion of Afghanistan. In July 1979, NSA reviewed all its past intelligence in Cuba and discovered that it had information in its files pertaining to a Soviet "brigade" in Cuba. Subsequent collection and analysis concluded that the unit in Cuba was indeed a Soviet combat unit, and this information was published in a CIA NID and promptly leaked to the press. The Senate postponed a scheduled hearing on treaty ratification until the Soviets agreed to withdraw the unit. The Soviets refused, and the Senate voted to suspend any debate on SALT II until President Carter could assure it that the unit did not have a combat role. The State Department subsequently discovered that the Soviet military unit had been in Cuba since the 1962 Cuban Missile Crisis with State Department approval, but the damage had been done.[11]

Soviet Invasion of Afghanistan

On 25 December 1979, the Soviets invaded Afghanistan, and all consideration of ratification of the Salt II Treaty ceased when Carter withdrew the treaty from the Senate. The Carter administration was deeply upset by the Soviet action and severely criticized CIA for its failure to warn of the massive invasion, which involved several Soviet divisions. MacEachin was on the Strategic Warning Staff at the Pentagon at the time, where he had been heavily involved in monitoring the Soviet troop buildup since early May. He has written a detailed account of how the IC closely monitored the Soviet military preparations but failed to predict the scale of the actual invasion.[12] He blamed the mindset of CIA intelligence analysts who, in the absence of hard evidence, failed to correctly estimate Soviet intentions by using their own US rationale for what the Soviets might do. MacEachin states that the invasion was a major intelligence warning failure because of so-called "mirror imaging."[13]

Gates, who was at the NSC at the time, was kinder to CIA in his description of its intelligence input. According to Gates, Arnold Horelick, then NIO for the Soviet Union, was a political expert, not a military one, and he focused on the intentions of the Soviet political leadership. Horelick began to warn of a potential Soviet military intervention as early as March 1979 and, with input from military analysts in OSR, continued to monitor the military preparations. In September, Turner sent an alert memorandum to the President stating that Soviet leaders might be on the threshold of a decision to commit combat forces but assessing that the intervention would be an incremental one. Turner sent another alert memo on 19 December, which reported a substantial buildup of Soviet combat units on the border and the potential for major reinforcements. NSA gave final warnings of a major Soviet intervention on 22 and 24 December, hours before some 85,000 troops began to pour into Afghanistan. Gates concluded that CIA tracked the growing Soviet involvement in Afghanistan with great precision and conveyed it to policymakers in a timely manner, including providing good tactical warning of the actual invasion, but he faulted CIA's political analysts for failing to understand that Brezhnev might be foolish enough to actually invade.[14]

From the perspective of MacEachin and other military analysts in OSR, the major problem leading to such intelligence failures, as was the case with the Soviet invasion of Czechoslovakia in 1968, was getting accurate intelligence on Soviet political intentions in crises. Turner gave much credit to the ability of skilled CIA military analysts to monitor Soviet military deployments and capabilities, but the difficult part—determining Soviet leadership intentions—was left primarily to political analysts. Howard Stoertz would probably agree that better political analysis was needed to determine Soviet leadership intentions, especially because Stoertz believed that a lack of good political input on Soviet strategic intentions was a major problem with the A-Team/B-team exercise in 1976.[15]

Soviet Strategic Forces NIEs

After the Soviet invasion of Afghanistan, Turner began to take an even stronger hand in overseeing CIA estimates on Soviet strategic forces and intentions.[16] The result was NIE 11-3/8-79, *Soviet Capabilities for Strategic Nuclear Conflict Through the 1980s*, issued in March 1980, several months after the Soviet invasion of Afghanistan. Like its immediate predecessor, the NIE was published in three volumes. The first volume was a summary, the second the actual estimate, and the third was a detailed annex. Turner took a direct hand in the drafting of the summary volume, and the tone of the estimate was significantly more somber than the previous one done before the Soviet invasion. Nevertheless, DIA and all the military service intelligence organizations took a footnote to the statement that Soviet leaders still saw the strategic situation as one of nuclear parity and mutual deterrence. The Pentagon saw the Soviets as perceiving that the situation was one of the Soviets' own growing nuclear superiority and that there was a distinct danger that the Soviet leadership might miscalculate US reactions during a regional crisis "and thus set the stage for a serious military confrontation between the superpowers."

In addition, Turner again included what he called a "quasi-dynamic analysis of Soviet and US intercontinental strike forces." These were projected estimates of the residual Soviet and US strategic forces that would survive a first ICBM strike by either side. Again, the Pentagon took an alternative view that such residual analysis produces misleading results with respect to trends in the strategic balance and nuclear deterrence, and that it "comprises a net assessment from the US perspective which is not a proper function of intelligence." Therefore, DIA and the military services stated that the residual analysis should be removed from the estimate and that such net assessments should be left to DoD. Turner responded with his own statement as DCI. He said that it would be a disservice to national decision-makers to remove the quasi-dynamic analysis because it was important to those who see mutual residual destruction as the key ingredient of deterrence. In a final retort, DIA and the military services took a footnote to disassociate themselves from the entire summary of the estimate.

This was strong stuff indeed. As a result, the 1980 Soviet strategic NIE was a significant departure from past practices. Issued in December 1980 as NIE 11-3/8-80, *Soviet Capabilities for Strategic Nuclear Conflict Through 1990*, it was Turner's swan song as DCI on the Soviet military threat to US strategic interests. The NIE was unprecedented in that it contained two sets of key judgments: one was the usual version coordinated by the Intelligence Community; the other was written by DCI Turner himself. To compare the strategic capabilities of both sides, Turner again used a net assessment approach to conclude that a rough parity existed despite a growing Soviet advantage in some areas, such as total numbers of delivery vehicles. However, Turner judged that the residual strategic nuclear forces of both sides after a surprise attack would likely be sufficient for the Soviets to see a nuclear conflict as a very high risk, and that the Soviets would almost certainly prefer nuclear arms limitations to a strategic arms race with the United States. The high costs of such an arms race would be a major factor in Soviet considerations because of declining industrial productivity and the magnitude of the Soviet Union's forthcoming economic problems.

In effect, the DCI key judgments and summary of the NIE became the CIA version, which was produced with heavy input from OSR and OSWR. The key judgments used the royal "we" and contained no alternative views. As a result, the coordinated Community version contained only the alternative views of the State Department and DoD. In almost every case, the DIA and military service alternatives were more alarmist than the main text, and the State version less so. For example, while the main text stated that some Soviet leaders might hold the view that victory in a nuclear war was possible, the State Department's alternative view was that "victory" was a Soviet ideological concept, not an objective goal of Soviet policy. The DoD alternative view was that the Soviet concept of a military and political victory was real and called for the survival of a Soviet communist political entity, the strategic and military neutralization of the United States, and the seizure and occupation of Europe. In addition, DoD again took exception to the use of US strategic force data to do a comparison of Soviet and US offensive forces, stating that although the US forces data was provided by the Office of the Secretary of Defense, it had no official status and therefore should not be used in the estimate.

The 1980 Soviet strategic forces estimate was the swan song not only for DCI Turner, but also for NIO for Strategic Programs Howard Stoertz. Stoertz had an extremely busy year in 1980, not only overseeing his last NIE 11-3/8 but two other key estimates as well. One was NIE 11-12-80, *Prospects for Soviet Military Technology and R&D*, and the other was NIE 11-1-80, *Soviet Military Capabilities and Intentions in Space.*[17] Both were highly technical estimates done with heavy inputs from OSWR and OSR. The Soviet military technology estimate was the more controversial of the two. It provided an assessment of Soviet prospects for military technology and R&D, as well as the relative US and Soviet standings in key military technologies. DIA took a footnote to the assessment of the relative standings of the two countries in 16 key military technologies, arguing that the IC was not well equipped to render such a comparison, and DIA provided an alternative assessment with a number of exceptions from the general estimate. DCI Turner took a footnote of his own, challenging the general view that the Soviet military sector was isolated from the problems of the economy as a whole. In contrast, the Soviet military space estimate was non-controversial, even though it stated that US space satellite technology was more advanced than Soviet satellite systems.

Stoertz Retires

After 32 years of service in CIA, which began in late 1948, Stoertz decided to retire in mid-1980. In a subsequent interview, he gave several reasons for the decision.[18] First, Stoertz said that the job was becoming more difficult because the period of detente and arms control with the Soviet Union was ending and the period of strategic military confrontation was beginning. Furthermore, with the failure to ratify SALT II, it was getting harder to do ten-year projections of future Soviet strategic nuclear capabilities without doing net assessments. Stoertz added that this process was becoming more difficult because cooperation with DoD was declining. Finally, Stoertz said that while he had great respect for Turner, now that the DCI was writing his own estimates, the job was less fun. At Stoertz's retirement, Turner presented him with the Distinguished Intelligence Medal, and in 1997 Stoertz was selected as one of CIA's Trailblazers for his pioneering intelligence support to arms control policymakers. He was also noted as the first director of the Imagery Analysis Service, the first chief of the SALT Support Staff, and the first national intelligence officer for strategic programs.

Frank Ruocco, who worked closely with Stoertz for five years in OSR's Strategic Forces Division, remembers Stoertz as the one individual who had more analytical rigor and integrity than anyone else in the Agency. During this time frame, Stoertz was heavily involved in intelligence support to the SALT negotiations, participating in the A-Team/B-Team exercise, and overseeing the production of Soviet strategic military estimates. Ruocco said that Stoertz did not go through the chain of command to get intelligence input; rather, Stoertz would call Ruocco and other senior Agency officers directly all the time. Ruocco said the period was exhausting but exhilarating because OSR was doing a lot of meaningful work.[19]

Gorman and Net Assessments

Stoertz was not the only NIO who supported net assessments and lamented the lack of DoD cooperation. The NIO for general purpose

Soviet BM-21 (multiple rocket launcher).

forces from May 1979 to April 1980 was Army Maj. Gen. Paul Gorman. Gorman was responsible for producing a secret version of NIE 11-14-79, *Warsaw Pact Forces Opposite NATO*, which had been issued in a top secret version in January 1979 in support of the ongoing MBFR negotiations. Both versions were done with considerable input from OSR's Theater Forces Division, and both went into considerable detail on the Warsaw Pact ground, air, and naval forces opposite NATO, including those forces in the western Soviet Union. The estimates also included sections on Pact policy and doctrine, strategy, and theater nuclear forces. What the estimates lacked, however, was any comparison of the capabilities of Warsaw Pact forces in Eastern Europe with those of NATO forces in Western Europe.

In a long article that Gorman wrote in late 1979, he regretted the fact that while policymakers wanted to see such a comparison of the balance of forces, and that such a force comparison was done in the NIE 11-3/8 series of estimates on the strategic balance, this was not the case in the Warsaw Pact estimates.[20] Gorman put the blame squarely on DIA and the military services, both of which he said blocked any attempt to include a net assessment of how the Warsaw Pact stacked up militarily against NATO. Gorman noted that OSR had published a study, *The Balance of Forces in Central Europe*, in August 1977 which made such a comparison, and he stated it was time for the Intelligence Community to do likewise in a national intelligence estimate. Gorman was not able to accomplish this, however, before he departed in April 1980. DCI Turner awarded Gorman the National Intelligence Distinguished Service Medal soon after. Gorman's career did not suffer because of his criticism of DoD. As it turned out, he left to become director of policy and plans on the Army Staff and was then appointed as CINCSOUTH and promoted to lieutenant general.

OSR's Accomplishments

During the 1979–80 period, OSR's Theater Forces Division under Ben Rutherford continued to contribute to various interagency products done in support of the SALT II treaty effort or the MBFR talks, even though both were stalled. These included several IIMs on NATO force modernization, an assessment of Warsaw Pact manpower in the MBFR force reduction area, and a series of papers on European theater nuclear forces that might be useful in future arms limitation talks. The data on theater nuclear forces was developed by an interagency working group that Aris Pappas of OSR headed under the direction of the Arms Control Intelligence Staff (ACIS). ACIS was created in January 1980 under NFAC and was originally led by Ray McCrory. Several OSR analysts served under the staff at various times until March 1989, when ACIS was transferred to the DCI area. The first three chiefs of ACIS under the DCI were Doug MacEachin, Craig Chellis, and John Lauder—all former OSR military analysts.

The Eastern Forces Division of OSR under Robert Will was also busy during 1979–80. It contributed heavily to NIE 35/36-80, *The Arab-Israeli Military Balance, 1980-1985*, issued in August 1980. This was an updated version of the 1977 estimate on the same topic and was another massive work published in two volumes. Its key judgments were that Israel had continued to increase its margin of military superiority over its Arab adversaries since the 1973 war and was capable of defeating them on any all fronts.

The Military-Economic Analysis Center under Don Burton continued to provide substantial intelligence inputs to the various Soviet military estimates done during the 1979–80 time frame. James Barry was chief of the Economics Implications Branch, which provided the contributions on Soviet military defense spending for the estimates, particularly the NIE 11-3/8 series. These contributions continued to state that Soviet leaders were clearly concerned about the slowing growth of the Soviet economy, which was projected to decline further in the early 1980s, and that nothing indicated that the Soviets were considering significant cuts in defense spending.[21]

In addition to the defense spending inputs for Soviet military estimates, MEAC also continued to provide material on current and projected Soviet defense spending to DoD budget planners. For example, in September 1979, Huffstutler sent a MEAC contribution to the Pentagon for its annual posture statement on defense development for research and engineering. The input, titled "The Soviet Defense Buildup," focused on Soviet resources devoted to research, development, testing, and engineering. It also examined Soviet force developments for each major military component during the previous years and compared the costs to those of similar US force programs. Two other detailed studies that MEAC produced in 1979 and 1980 examined the trend in Soviet defense spending and the expansion of Soviet defense industries since the mid-1960s, each with projections for the next decade taking into account then current Soviet economic difficulties.[22]

Like Sayre Stevens before him, Bruce Clarke was a big advocate of joint NFAC working groups designed to coordinate research and analysis of high-priority intelligence issues. Soon after Clarke became D/NFAC, Huffstutler had OSR take the lead in doing a major review of the growth of Soviet military power since Brezhnev had come to power and to forecast its likely development over the next decade. According to Huffstutler, the study was to include the political and economic dimensions of Soviet military power as well, with major inputs from other NFAC offices. It took two years to prepare; the final product was designed to be a primer for the next administration, which turned out to be that of President Ronald Reagan.

The resulting intelligence assessment, titled *The Development of Soviet Military Power: Trends Since 1965 and Prospects for the 1980s*, was issued in April 1981.[23] In breadth, scope, and detail, it matched or exceeded anything CIA had done previously, including the Soviet military NIEs. It was a massive study of about 175 pages and drew on the contributions of 40 separate intelligence products from every component in NFAC. The assessment included three appendices: one of NFAC publications related to the study, another on biographies of key Soviet military policy figures, and the last on characteristics of major Soviet weapons systems. An NFAC Working Group chaired by James Barry of OSR—which included members from the Offices of Political Analysis, Economic Analysis, Scientific and Weapons Research, and

Imagery Analysis—oversaw the research effort and produced the final report.

The assessment was a comprehensive and somber look at the impressive growth of Soviet military power since Brezhnev had come to power. This growth was driven by the continued increase in Soviet defense spending, which by 1980 consumed over one-eighth of GNP. The study then sounded a note of caution about future Soviet defense spending, based on a domestic economy whose growth had slowed to a crawl in the previous few years. The annual rise in GNP in 1979 and 1980 was only a little over one percent, the worst since World War II. Consequently, unless defense spending slowed significantly, fewer funds would be available for the civilian economy, including agriculture, industry, and transportation. The study added that the pending political succession of an aging Soviet President Brezhnev would further complicate the problem that Soviet leaders would have in allocating economic resources in the ensuing decade.

The assessment then discussed several alternative projections of Soviet military power in the 1980s. The baseline projection assumed that despite growing economic concerns, Soviet leaders would continue to allocate enough resources to defense spending to prevent any significant effect on military capabilities, although some adjustments were likely. After going into considerable detail about what this would mean for the growth of Soviet strategic and theater forces—including the missile, ground, air and naval components—the study offered two alternative projections. The first was the possibility that the Soviets would reduce the level of military expenditures absolutely, not just reduce the rate of their increase. This was judged unlikely because Soviet leaders had a dim view of the international environment and because of the lack of evidence of any planned cuts in defense spending. The second alternative was for a more rapid growth in defense spending, which was also considered unlikely. The study concluded that the Soviet leadership would prefer, if possible, to keep defense expenditures within the then current growth rate. The IC judged that meanwhile, the Soviets would seek to constrain US military force growth by urging further arms control negotiations and by attempting to undermine Western cohesiveness on defense issues.

The assessment was not completed before DCI Turner left office and never received much attention under the new Reagan administration. It was a well-integrated and noncontentious look at the political and economic considerations that Soviet leaders would have to deal with in shaping future military policy, including various international factors such as the Chinese military threat and considerable instability in the Third World. The final product was a good example of what the various functional offices in NFAC could achieve when they produced a truly joint study. It went well beyond the previous Soviet strategic military estimate produced under Turner in its consideration of the political and economic factors likely to influence Soviet military policy in the 1980s. It even mentioned Mikhail Gorbachev as one of the potential candidates to succeed Brezhnev when the aging ruler eventually left the scene.

Turner's Legacy

Turner had hoped to stay on as DCI in the new Reagan administration, according to Richard Lehman, and Turner even insisted on personally briefing Reagan both before and after the election. Once it was clear that William Casey was Reagan's choice for DCI, Clarke suggested to Lehman that Kerr and his deputy chief of the Office of Current Operations, Dixon Davis, brief President Reagan, which they did. In late December 1980, Casey contacted Clarke and Lehman and asked for a meeting to get acquainted, but he declined the standard intelligence briefings before his confirmation, stating that he already understood the key issues concerning CIA. Lehman added that indeed Casey did understand the key intelligence issues and that he already had strong ideas about what needed to be done.[24]

Turner's legacy as DCI was mixed at best, but those military analysts in OSR who worked closely with the DCI on the Soviet Bloc military estimates generally viewed Turner positively, primarily because of his strong interest in the subject matter and his willingness to take on DIA and the military services. Frank Ruocco, who worked very closely with Turner, said that the DCI was very interested in the analytic product and process and that he liked Turner and enjoyed their discussions.

Ruocco said that Turner would accept argument and not dictate his own position, although he was not shy about expressing his opinion, especially in the Soviet strategic forces estimates.[25] Turner himself has said that he appreciated the great ability of CIA military analysts to piece together many small pieces of information with no evident policy bias.

Those higher up the chain of command—including Sayre Stevens, Richard Lehman, and Bruce Clarke—had more mixed views. They believed that the creation of NFAC to oversee analysis in the Intelligence Community never worked out and that Turner's selection of Robert Bowie as NFAC's first director was a bad choice. Stevens thought that making him the ADDI diminished his former role as the DDI and stated that this contributed to his decision to retire in early 1979. Lehman, whom Bowie replaced as deputy director to the DCI for national intelligence, became the NIO for warning and had little to say that was positive about either Turner or Bowie. Lehman helped convince Turner to replace Bowie with Clarke. Clarke got along well with Turner but thought he was taking too much of a direct role in the Soviet strategic estimates and was making the process much too complicated. Clarke also thought that the estimates themselves were getting too long and lacked focus and that the process needed to be changed. He tried to get Turner to abolish NFAC and go back to the DDI structure, but Turner refused. Nevertheless, Clarke said that Turner was always a gentleman and willing to listen to criticism, and he acknowledges Turner's strong interest in intelligence analysis.[26]

❖ ❖ ❖

Endnotes

1. Robert M. Huffstutler, interviewed by James Hanrahan, 29 May 2002.
2. Clarke, interviewed by Hanrahan, 29 May 2002.
3. Richard Kerr, interviewed by James Hanrahan, 7 September 2002.
4. "OSR Organization," 3 May 1979.

5. Gates's *From the Shadows* provides an insider's look at President Carter's foreign policy actions during his final two years in office.

6. Ibid., 116.

7. Ibid., 122.

8. Ibid., 113–117.

9. Turner, Secrecy and Democracy, 235–241.

10. Gates, *From the Shadows*, 115–116.

11. Ibid., 155–161.

12. Doug MacEachin, *Predicting the Soviet Invasion of Afghanistan: the Intelligence Community's Record*, www.cia.gov/library, Center for the Study of Intelligence.

13. MacEachin, interviewed by Dietel, 13 July 2007.

14. Gates, *From the Shadows*, 131–134.

15. Stoertz, interviewed by Hanrahan, 8 May 1998.

16. Garthoff, "Estimating Soviet Strategic Military Intentions and Capabilities," 169–170 provides details on DCI Turner's role in drafting these two estimates. They are available in Steury, *Intentions and Capabilities*, 407–466.

17. NIE 11-12-80, *Prospects for Soviet Military Technology and R&D*, 31 July 1980; and NIE 11-1-80, *Soviet Military Capabilities and Intentions in Space*, 8 August 1980.

18. Stoertz, interviewed by Hanrahan, 8 May 1998.

19. Holmes, interviewed by Dietel, 3 June 2009.

20. Paul F. Gorman, "Measuring the Military Balance in Central Europe," in CIA, CSI, *Studies in Intelligence*, Winter 1979, 1-37.

21. OSR/MEAC, contribution to NIE 11-3/8-78, 21 July 1978. OSR intelligence reports during this period are located in the CIA Archives, Job 96S01330R, Box 7 of 8, Folder 8.

22. Ibid.

23. A summary of the report, SR 81-100-35X, April 1981 is available in Haines and Leggett, *CIA's Analysis of the Soviet Union*, 1947–1997, 295–310.

24. Lehman, interviewed by Kovar, 29 February 1998.

25. Ruocco, interviewed by Drewyer, 9 May 2006.

26. Clarke, interviewed by Hanrahan, 25 April 2002.

❖ ❖ ❖

Chapter Nine: 1981 and Beyond

The Casey Era Begins and the Demise of OSR and Its Legacy

William Casey's arrival at CIA was awaited with some trepidation, primarily because of his reputation as a hardline conservative and a member of the Committee on the Present Danger (CPD). But whereas other members of the CPD, particularly those who had supported the Team B report in 1976, wanted to dismember or purge CIA, Casey wanted to revitalize and rebuild it. Casey had been a wartime member of the OSS; his hero was William Donovan, who founded the OSS in 1942. As DCI, Casey commissioned a statue of Donovan that was placed inside CIA Headquarters in 1988, after Casey's death. Casey agreed to take the DCI position when President Reagan said it would have cabinet status; he was keen to take the job. Casey believed that he could improve CIA's morale, which he thought had suffered during the Carter administration. At his first staff meeting at CIA soon after his confirmation, Casey repudiated the 1976 Team-B report, stating that his role was to make CIA a stronger and more effective intelligence service. Furthermore, the staff all knew that Casey had cabinet status and the ear of President Reagan, whom he called "Ron," and that he was close to Richard Allen, the new national security advisor.[1]

Casey's deputy was a career military intelligence officer, Admiral Bobby Ray Inman, who had been director of NSA when Casey was selected for the DCI job. Casey did not pick Inman personally; Inman was planning to retire and initially did not want the job. However, Senator Barry Goldwater (R-AZ), who had become the new head of the Senate Intelligence Oversight Committee, wanted Inman as Casey's deputy.

President Reagan finally persuaded Inman to take the deputy DCI position, but Inman only agreed to stay on for 18 months. Inman and Casey never got along, however, and Inman resigned after only a little more than a year in the job. Soon after Inman arrived, Casey promoted Gates from his position as the NIO for the USSR and Eastern Europe to the director of the newly created DCI/DDCI Executive Staff.

Casey's Agenda

Unlike Turner, Casey had little interest in his role as director of the Intelligence Community. He focused on running CIA, especially the analytic and covert action sides. Casey strongly believed that the Agency's mission was to help the Reagan administration confront the growing global power and influence of the Soviet Union. He wanted CIA's analysis to be more sharply focused and relevant to policymakers, and he wanted the collection and covert action side of the business to be more aggressive and far-reaching. Also unlike Turner, Casey had no plans to impose a large-scale turnover of CIA's senior managers. The only senior person that Casey brought with him to CIA was Max Hugel, whom Casey initially named to fill the vacant DDA position.

Nevertheless, within a few months of Casey's arrival, the senior leadership of both NFAC and the clandestine service changed. The first to go was Bruce Clarke as head of NFAC. Clarke said that when he asked Casey about his future as a holdover from the Carter administration, Casey said that he wanted Clarke to stay on. However, Clarke said that he had trouble accommodating Casey's views on how to run analysis and that by March 1981, he had told the DCI that he wanted to resign for personal reasons. Clarke added that his new Austrian wife wanted him to retire so they could both return to Vienna to take care of her ill father, which Clarke did after Casey accepted his resignation.[2]

Casey's biographer, Joseph Persico, tells a somewhat different story. Persico said that Casey was unhappy with the intelligence that NFAC produced because it was not relevant to the needs of the new administration, and that the DCI told Clarke this directly. Casey was particularly unhappy about the Soviet estimates—which he thought were too cautious in reaching conclusions about Soviet intentions— and he believed that Clarke was not the one to bring about change. In any case, by April 1981, Clarke was gone, and Casey replaced him with John McMahon, who was then the current DDO. Evans Hineman stayed on as McMahon's deputy at NFAC. In a surprise move, Casey then replaced McMahon as DDO with Max Hugel, a change that turned out to be a disaster and lasted only two months.[3]

The next to go was Richard Lehman, the chairman of the NIC. Casey recruited Henry Rowen from the RAND Corporation to take over that position in July 1981. Lehman agreed to stay on as Rowen's deputy for another year until his retirement. Casey was adamant that he wanted the estimates to be done quickly and to reach clear conclusions, and if a consensus could not be reached, he wanted the Community to lay out the key differences. Casey wanted the estimates to help drive administration policy, and he picked up the pace of estimative production substantially.[4]

Almost immediately after he arrived, Casey ordered a quick update of the last estimate done on Soviet global goals, which had been issued in 1978. Done as a Memorandum to Holders, M/H NIE 11-4-78, *Soviet Goals and Expectations in the Global Power Arena,* was published in July 1981. Unlike the previous estimate, which emphasized Soviet strategic military policy, the update focused on Soviet efforts to gain a dominant position in the Third World. It portrayed a Soviet leadership that was assertive and confident despite an approaching succession crisis and a stagnating economy. It paid particular attention to Soviet gains in the Arab world—especially Syria, Libya, and South Yemen—as well as new Soviet successes in Latin America, including Cuba and Nicaragua.

Casey was obsessed with the expansion of Soviet and Cuban power and influence in Central America. He viewed the Sandinistas in Nicaragua as Soviet/Cuban surrogates and was convinced that both countries were determined to support leftist insurgent groups throughout the region, especially in El Salvador. He ordered a series of intelligence estimates on the looming Soviet and Cuban threat in the region, with a special focus on Central America and Sandinista support to the leftist insurgency in El Salvador, which had become a US client state.[5]

OSR Reorganization

In response to Casey's heightened concern about Soviet military activities in Latin America and Africa, Rae Huffstutler decided to reorganize OSR again. Announced in April 1981, it was the first major structural change in the office since 1977 and was designed to put more military analytic focus on the Third World, particularly Latin America and Africa.[6] The top leadership of OSR remained Huffstutler and his deputy Frank Reynolds, with Joan Phelan as the executive officer. (See chart opposite).

The first major change was in the former Eastern Forces Division, renamed the Regional Forces Division. Robert Will and Mark Detweiler still led the division. The China and Asian Forces Branches remained unchanged, but the former Middle East/North Africa Branch was expanded to cover South Asia and renamed the Near East/South Asia Branch. This expansion was designed to put more focus on Afghanistan and the India-Pakistan military balance. In addition, a fourth branch, the Latin America/African Forces Branch, was added to the division. It concentrated on the Soviet and Cuban military presence in both Africa and Latin America as well as the status of key leftist insurgencies in each region. The branch chiefs were Frank O'Hara for Asian Forces, Mikel Goodwin for China Forces, Morgan Jones for Near East/South Asia, and David Johnson for Latin America/Africa.

The next change was in the former Regional Analysis Division, which was renamed the Current Analysis Division. Jack Gains led it, with Robert Korn as his deputy. The division did current intelligence reporting, crisis response, and briefings on military developments worldwide. It was also responsible for coordinating intelligence exchanges with foreign intelligences services. It had three branches: USSR-Eastern Europe, Asian Forces, and Near East/Africa/Latin America. They were headed by Helen Reed, Wayne Wolfe, and David Christian respectively. Helen Reed was the first woman to achieve branch-chief level who had started her career in OSR, and her branch was given the task of producing the President's Quarterly Report (PQR) on Soviet Forces that had begun under President Nixon and continued through

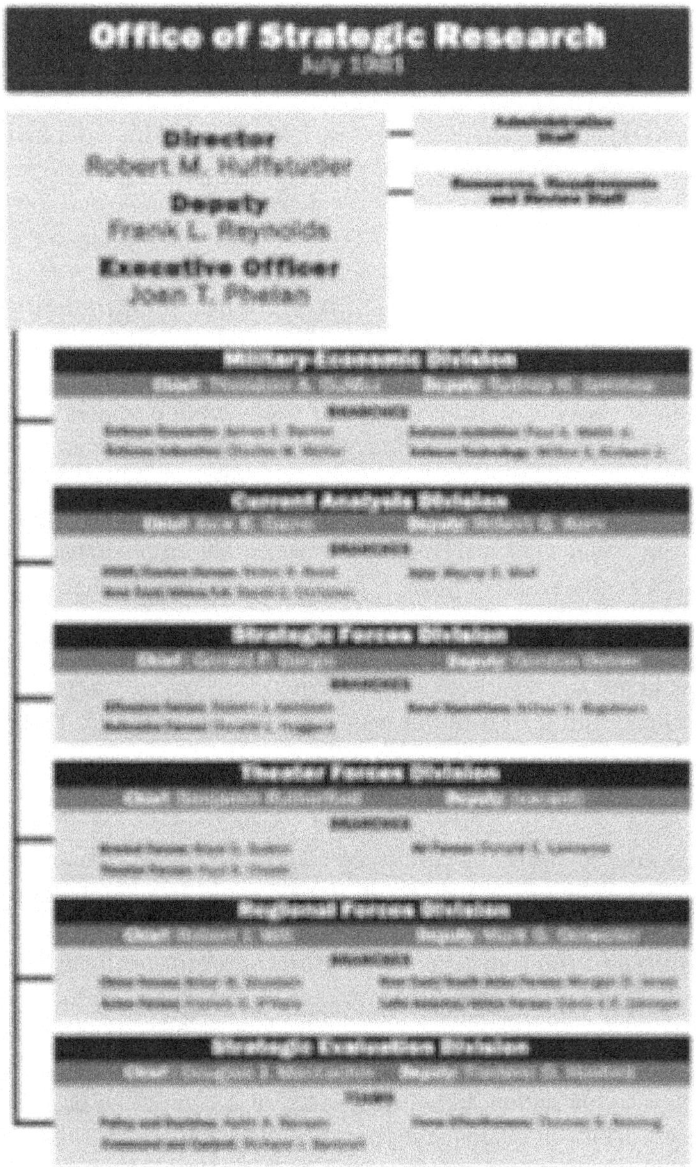
Office of Strategic Research
July 1981
Director
Robert M. Huffstutler
Deputy
Frank L. Reynolds
Executive Officer
Joan T. Phelan
Military-Economic Division
Current Analysis Division
Strategic Forces Division
Theater Forces Division
Regional Forces Division
Strategic Evaluation Division

the Carter administration. DCI Turner made it a net force assessment by including US forces as well, despite DoD objections.

The Strategic Forces Division remained organizationally unchanged, but by then it was headed by Gerald Dargis, with Gordon Oehler as his deputy. Dargis had returned from the National War College in 1980 and replaced Frank Ruocco as division chief. Huffstutler had sent Ruocco to become the deputy director of OIA under Wayne Strand. Strand in turn had replaced Noel Firth as head of OIA, and Firth returned to CIA Headquarters to work on community affairs for Bruce Clarke at NFAC. The Strategic Forces Division still had three branches: Offensive Missiles, Defensive Missile, and Naval Operations. They were led by Robert Ashdown, Donald Hoggard, and Arthur Begelman respectively. The division focused primarily on the Soviet Union but division analysts also did research on other foreign strategic missile programs as well as on naval forces that the Regional Forces Division did not cover. It also continued to provide strategic intelligence for potential arms control negotiations. An Arms Control Intelligence Staff had been established in NFAC in January 1980 under Bruce Clarke, and OSR analysts were sent there on rotation to support it.

The Theater Forces Division continued to be headed by Ben Rutherford, who remained without a deputy when Ted DuMez was reassigned to the new Military-Economic Division. The Ground and Air Forces Branches remained unchanged, but the former Western Forces Branch was renamed the Theater Operations Branch. The branch chiefs were Boyd Sutton, Donald Lawrence, and Alan Rehm respectively. The ground and air branches continued to monitor developments in the ground, air, and air defense forces of the Soviet Bloc countries as well as those of Western Europe. The new Theater Operations Branch was responsible for focusing on the doctrines, procedures, and capabilities of both West European and Warsaw Pact forces to conduct theater warfare, including the use of nuclear, biological, and chemical weapons. It also followed trends in the conventional force balance and force readiness in the region. Finally, the division continued to be the focal point in CIA for intelligence support to the MBFR negotiations.

In addition to the changes in the existing divisions, both the former Military-Economic Analysis and Strategic Evaluation Centers were converted to standard divisions and renamed accordingly. The Military Economic Division was then headed by Ted DuMez, who replaced Don Burton, and Sydney Jammes succeeded John Reynolds as his deputy. The division dealt with the defense budgets and programs of all communist countries as well as comparisons with US defense spending and was organized into four branches. The Defense Activities Branch did aggregate comparisons of Soviet and US defense activities—including manpower, military equipment, and weapons production—and also estimated Chinese defense expenditures. The Defense Economic Branch did estimates of the economic burden of Soviet defense spending in Western economic terms and as perceived by the Soviets, as well as the economic considerations of Warsaw Pact defense programs. The Defense Industries Branch was responsible for in-depth analysis of the organization and development of Soviet defense industries, including R&D programs. The Defense Technology Branch performed weapon systems cost analyses by developing dollar-cost models of Soviet weapons, often with contractual support. The branch chiefs were Paul Welsh for Defense Activities, James Steiner for Defense Economic, Charles Walter for Defense Industries, and Wilber Rickard for Defense Technology. The Analytic Support Group was led by Robert Shefner.

Finally, Douglas MacEachin continued to head the Strategic Evaluation Division and Fred Hosford had replaced Gordon Oehler as his deputy. The division was responsible for political-military analysis, military doctrine analysis, and force effectiveness analysis for the Soviet Union and East European forces. It had a Policy and Doctrine Branch to analyze the various influences on Soviet military policy and doctrine, as well as to assess Soviet attitudes toward arms control, Soviet perceptions of foreign military developments, Soviet reactions to US military activities, and the Soviet military decisionmaking process. The Command and Control Branch did research on Soviet and Warsaw Pact command-and-control systems and provided indications and warning during crises. The Force Effectiveness Branch developed measures of effectiveness for Soviet strategic and theater forces to assess how the Soviets would wage a nuclear conflict. Keith Hansen led the branch for Policy and Doctrine, Richard Bardzell for Command and Control, and Thomas Behling for Force Effectiveness.

Military Intelligence Research and Production

During the next six months, OSR continued working at a heavy pace to do military intelligence research and production under Huffstutler's leadership, much of which DCI Casey personally requested. Most of the publications were SNIEs, which were shorter and more focused than the longer Soviet strategic estimates in the 11-3/8 series and could be produced relatively quickly. One of the first was SNIE 11-4/2-81, *Soviet Potential to Respond to US Strategic Force Improvements, and Foreign Reactions*, issued in October 1981. It was noteworthy primarily because it essentially was a net assessment of potential US and Soviet strategic force developments, and it included the same Pentagon footnote that DIA and the military intelligence services had taken to DCI Turner's inclusion of net assessments in previous Soviet strategic NIEs. This was the last net assessment done under Casey, however, because the DCI subsequently agreed to leave net force Soviet/US force assessments to DoD.

Other Soviet-related SNIEs issued during this period that OSR contributed to include *The Soviet Threat to Pakistan* and *the Dependence of Soviet Military Power on Economic Relations With the West.*[7] In addition, a number of IIMs were also issued on Soviet military issues pertaining to NATO. These included one on Soviet capabilities to interdict sea lines of communication in a conflict with NATO, one on the assessed manpower of Warsaw Pact forces in the MBFR reduction area, and another on theater nuclear forces in Europe.[8]

In addition to these Community products, OSR continued to produce its own research reports, provide input to arms control efforts, issue current intelligence reports, and help staff crisis task forces. Two such tasks forces were in existence throughout 1981. One monitored the Soviet conflict in Afghanistan, and the other tracked the continuing political crisis in Poland. The Reagan administration was greatly concerned about potential Soviet and Warsaw Pact military intervention in Poland if Solidarity continued to challenge the military regime that took power there in early February 1981. The crisis did not ease until December 1981 when the military government, at the urging of Moscow, imposed martial law and arrested many Solidarity leaders and other political opponents.

DI Reorganization

Casey liked the concept of such task forces because they provided him with a single point of contact on key issues rather than necessitating that he deal with several different offices. As a result, Casey asked John McMahon soon after McMahon took over as D/NFAC in April 1981 to consider establishing a Soviet analysis center that would combine political, economic, and military analysts from OPA, OER, and OSR into a single component. Huffstutler and others within NFAC opposed the idea, however, because it would have required pulling analysts from the existing functional offices and caused coordination problems. McMahon instead proposed a complete reorganization of the DI by breaking up the functional offices and creating regional ones.[9]

According to Huffstutler, Casey liked McMahon's proposal because most CIA customers—such as the NSC, State, and DoD—were organized along regional lines, thus they could have a single point of contact in CIA. McMahon created a task force that included representatives from OSR, OPA, and OER to study the problem. Doug MacEachin, the OSR member, remembers that a decision was made not to include OSWR in the regional mix, primarily because it was newly established and able to support all new regional offices.[10] The plan was to create five regional offices: Soviet Analysis (SOVA), European Analysis (EURA), East Asian Pacific Analysis (OEA), Near Eastern and South Asian Analysis (NESA), and African and Latin American Analysis (ALA). Another new office, the Office of Global Issues (OGI), was created to cover global issues. The offices left intact besides OSWR and OIA were the Office of Current Operations (OCO), which became the Office of Current Production and Analytic Support (CPAS) in March 1982, and the Office of Central Reference (OCR). The Office of Geographic and Societal Issues was also abolished along with OSR, OER, and OPA.

SOVA

With Casey's approval, McMahon announced in August 1981 that the reorganization would take effect on 1 October.[11] A major problem was consolidating the new offices into individual spaces. The largest new office by far would be SOVA, primarily because it included the Eastern European countries that were part of the Soviet Bloc. McMahon selected Huffstutler as the new director of SOVA with Douglas Dimon, the former deputy director of OER, as his deputy. McMahon then ordered Huffstutler to move his new office into a separate building outside of the CIA headquarters compound to make space available for the other new offices. Huffstutler admitted that the move was unpopular, but he undoubtedly wanted to help McMahon implement the massive reorganization as quickly and efficiently as possible. SOVA was not able to return to headquarters for three years.[12]

Once the move was complete, SOVA became by far the largest and most productive office in NFAC. Huffstutler recalls that it was a strong, well-balanced team producing about one third of the current intelligence reports and drafting 40 percent of the national estimates done in the early years of the Reagan administration. SOVA hit the ground running because most of the analysts in the existing OSR divisions, including Strategic Forces, Theater Forces, Military-Economic, and Strategic Evaluation, were transferred to SOVA almost intact. To this large cadre were added Soviet political, economic, and societal analysts from the former OPA and OER. Meanwhile, the military analysts in the Theater Forces Division who covered Western Europe ended up in EURA, and the analysts in the former Regional Forces and Current Analysis Divisions were sent to their corresponding new regional offices, with the bulk of them going to OEA and NESA. Only a few went to ALA.[13]

At the same time that McMahon announced the reorganization, he also named the new regional office leadership teams. In addition to Huffstutler, two other former OSR managers became new office directors, Richard Kerr for OEA and Frank Reynolds for ALA. Doug MacEachin became the deputy director of OCO under Dixon Davis, and Frank Ruocco remained as deputy director of OIA under Wayne

Strand. As a result, former OSR senior managers then led three of the five new regional offices, and two other DI offices had former OSR managers as deputy directors. This is a strong testament to the leadership skills and reputations that OSR officers had developed since Bruce Clarke first headed the office.

Gates Becomes D/NFAC

Soon after the NFAC reorganization took effect, McMahon began hinting that he wanted to retire. Casey did not want to lose him, however, and instead reestablished the position of CIA executive director, the number three leadership position in the Agency, and appointed McMahon to the position in January 1982 so he would stay on. Colby had abolished the position in September 1973 when he became DCI. This opened up the D/NFAC position, and Casey surprised almost everyone by picking Gates for the job rather than Hineman, who stayed on as Gates's deputy. At the same time, the name of the organization was changed back from NFAC to Directorate for Intelligence, as it was before Turner made the change in 1977. A year later, when Rowen left the NIC chairman position in September 1983 to return to teaching at Stanford University, Casey made Gates the new NIC chairman as well. These appointments demonstrated the high esteem that Casey had for Gates.[14]

The result was that Huffstutler was then working for a DDI whom he had brought into OSR as a senior manager in early 1980. Gates took a particular interest in all CIA analysis of the Soviet Union, and the two worked well together. Nevertheless, Gates's views of the Soviet Union were similar to Casey's, and he was a demanding and sometimes difficult boss. Meanwhile, Inman had decided to resign; when he left in June 1982, Casey replaced him with McMahon as DDCI. Soon after, Casey appointed Hineman as the new DS&T in July 1982 to replace Les Dirks, who had held the position since 1976. Kerr than replaced Hineman as Gates's ADDI. Thus Huffstutler was again working closely with both Gates and Kerr.

Clarke's Legacy of Leadership

One of the major legacies of Bruce Clarke's early strong leadership of OSR was the extraordinary number of former OSR analysts and managers who went on to hold senior positions in the Agency. Clarke knew them all well and was proud of their subsequent careers. They include the already mentioned John Hicks as head of NPIC and ADDI and Noel Firth as head of OIA. Although Gates served only briefly in OSR in 1979, he went on to select a large number of former OSR managers for senior positions in CIA during his tenures as DDI, DDCI, and DCI. Most notable were Kerr, who eventually became the deputy DCI in 1989, and Huffstutler, who rose to the number three position in CIA as executive director in 1992.

Kerr became Gates's deputy from July 1982 to January 1986 when Gates was the DDI. Kerr then briefly served as the DDA; when Gates became the deputy DCI under Casey in April 1986, he selected Kerr to replace as him as DDI. After Casey left office because of illness and was replaced as DCI by William Webster in March 1987, Gates stayed on as deputy DCI until March 1989. Kerr then became the deputy DCI from March 1989 to March 1992, first under William Webster and then under Gates when Gates returned to CIA as DCI in 1991. As for Huffstutler, in early 1984 DDS&T Hineman convinced him to leave SOVA and take over as director of NPIC, a position Huffstutler held until 1988. Huffstutler then served as deputy director for administration (DDA) from 1988 to 1992 under DCI Webster, and finally as the executive director of CIA under DCI Gates until Gates retired in 1993 and James Woolsey became DCI.

Other former OSR managers who went on to hold more senior positions in CIA include Fritz Ermarth, who had left the Agency in 1976 but returned as chairman of the NIC from 1988 to 1993. Doug MacEachin became the director of CPAS in 1983 and then replaced Huffstutler as D/SOVA in 1984. He became head of the DCI's Arms Control Intelligence Staff (ACIS) in 1989 and served as the DDI under Woolsey from 1993 to 1995. Frank Ruocco held a large number of senior positions. He was the head of the Collection Requirements and Evaluation Staff (CRES) from 1982 to 1986 and the chief of the Office of Collection

Resources (OCR), which became the Office of Information Resources (OIR), from 1985 to 1988. Ruocco then became director of NPIC from 1988 to 1991, following Huffstutler; headed the Office of Security from 1991 to 1992; and finally, became the DDA from 1992 to 1995, again following Huffstutler.

After OSR's demise in 1981, a number of other former OSR managers also became office or senior staff chiefs within the ensuing 15 years. These include Frank Reynolds, chief of both ALA and CPAS; Chris Holmes, director of both OSWR and OTI; Gordon Oehler, head of OSWR; Thomas Wolfe, chief of NESA; and Robert Vickers, head of OIA. In addition, both Craig Chellis and John Lauder followed MacEachin as head of ACIS, James Simon headed CRES, and both Omego Ware and John Dohring headed the Office of Equal Employment Opportunity (EEO). Too many other former OSR analysts to list separately went on to hold senior CIA positions during the subsequent few decades.

All of these future senior managers held Clarke in high esteem, and almost all tried to follow many of the management principles that Clarke had implemented when he was D/OSR and D/NFAC. These included getting to know the strengths and weaknesses of their subordinates and paying close attention to analysts' training and career development. Clarke also insisted on rigorous research and analysis, robust production, and careful editing. He knew his policy consumers and their major interests and intelligence needs well, and he ensured that the products he sent them had clear key judgments and supporting analysis. Clarke wanted his managers and analysts to work well with their CIA colleagues and know their counterparts in the IC. He also wanted them to understand intelligence collection capabilities, requirements, and gaps and to coordinate their analysis carefully within CIA and the rest of the IC if necessary. Finally, Clarke wanted them to produce intelligence reports not just for policymakers, but also to improve their own intelligence expertise and knowledge base.

Soviet Military Analysis Lives On

Regarding the legacy of OSR's military analysis after the office was abolished, SOVA had the largest number of former OSR analysts, and it continued to be the most productive of DI offices because of the high interest of the Reagan and Bush administrations in the Soviet Union up to and after its collapse. Gates had a strong personal interest in the Soviet Union and carefully reviewed all of SOVA's analytic products, including draft NIEs on all Soviet-related issues. After seven years at CIA from March 1982 to March 1989, first as the DDI and then as the DDCI, Gates then became an avid consumer of SOVA's intelligence output from 1989 to November 1991, when he moved to the White House to serve as deputy national security advisor under President Bush and National Security Advisor Brent Scowcroft. After Gates returned to CIA as the new DCI, he witnessed the collapse of the Soviet Union in December 1991 and remained at the Agency until January 1993.

Before the dissolution of the Soviet Union, SOVA played a very active role in providing intelligence support for arms control negotiations with the Soviet Union, drafting national intelligence estimates on Soviet military capabilities, and tracking Soviet defense spending. It was a time of political change in the Soviet Union and of continued Soviet economic problems, as well as of continued disagreements with the Pentagon on Soviet strategic military capabilities and intentions. Increasingly, SOVA's analysis of Soviet political, economic, military, and social trends took on a more pessimistic tone than those expressed in the NIEs. Huffstutler well remembers that in early 1982 SOVA produced a controversial study on Soviet weapons procurement since 1976 that concluded that little real growth had occurred in that sector of defense spending. The conclusion was at odds with a DIA study, and it caused a political uproar when it became known to Congress. Huffstutler had to participate in a DoD press conference to try to contain the political damage.

The End of the Cold War—and Military Analysis?

After the end of the Cold War, DCI Gates was forced to oversee the beginning of a dramatic reduction in the number of DI analysts working on the former Soviet Union. He was initially assisted in this effort by Kerr as his deputy and by Huffstutler as his executive director. The Cold War offices, which included SOVA, OSWR, and OIA, took the biggest cuts under the "peace dividend." SOVA, which was renamed the Office of Slavic and Eurasian Analysis (OSE) in 1992, eliminated over one third of its positions for military analysts, while the political and economic analysis cadre took smaller cuts. Gates and the DCI front office even considered the proposition that CIA no longer needed to retain a substantial capability to do conventional military force analysis and that perhaps much of this responsibility could be shifted to DoD. Although this was not done, the costing effort on the Russian defense budget was reduced dramatically, as was the training of new military analysts in the DI. In addition, OIA was merged with NPIC in 1993; when NPIC was transferred to DoD in 1996 by DCI John Deutch, CIA lost control its own imagery analysis capability. To most former OSR analysts, the collapse of the Soviet Union marked the beginning of the end of the era of robust independent military analysis in CIA.

❖ ❖ ❖

Endnotes

1. Casey's selection as DCI by President-elect Reagan and his first year in that office are covered in Persico, William J. Casey: From the OSS to the CIA, 200-252.
2. Bruce Clarke, interviewed by James Hanrahan, 25 April 2002.
3. Persico, Casey, 241-242.
4. Richard Lehman, interviewed by Richard Kovar, 29 February 1998.
5. "OSR Organization," 9 April 1981.
6. Rae Huffstutler, interviewed by James Hanrahan, 29 May 2002.

7. SNIE 11/32-81, The Soviet Threat to Pakistan, 12 August 1981; SNIE 3/11-4-81, Dependence of Soviet Military Power on Economic Relations with the West, 17 November 1981; and SNIE 11-4/2-81, Soviet Potential to Respond to US Strategic Nuclear Force Improvements and Foreign Relations, 6 October 1981.

8. NI IIM 81-100240x, Soviet Capabilities to Interdict Sea Lines of Communication in a Conflict with NATO, November 1981; NI IIM 81-10022, Assessed Manpower of Warsaw Pact Forces in the MBFR Reduction Area, October 1981; and NI IIM 81-10025, INF Support: Theater Nuclear Forces, December 1981.

9. Douglas MacEachin, interviewed by Edward Dietel, 13 July 2007.

10. NFAC Reorganization, 21 September 1981.

11. Rae Huffstutler, interviewed by James Hanrahan, 29 May 2002.

12. Persico, Casey, 294.

13. Rae Huffstutler, interviewed by James Hanrahan, 29 May 2002.

14. Persico, 294.

❖ ❖ ❖

Conclusion

Clearly, OSR made a major contribution to ensuring that CIA provided policymakers with vital strategic military intelligence support during the period of its existence and, through its legacy of strong leadership and analysis, up to the end of the Cold War. In his note to OSR on its fifth anniversary on 1 July 1972, DCI Richard Helms stated that not only was OSR's voice heard throughout the government but also that it was playing a vital role in arms control efforts:

> *In many ways, the past five years have been ones of preparation, of laying a foundation for future work. That work is taking shape even now as Congress considers the ABM treaty and the offensive systems agreement signed by the President in Moscow in May. The very possibility of agreements like these, or the ones that may come about on Warsaw Pact and NATO forces, turns in large part on the capability for systematic, careful, and accurate analysis and reporting that is the hallmark of OSR.*[1]

Later that year, National Security Advisor Henry Kissinger visited CIA on 18 September to celebrate the Agency's 25th anniversary. In his remarks, Kissinger noted that Helms had early on told him that in times of crisis, Kissinger would find that only one agency worked for the President alone, and that this had proven true. Kissinger then added:

> *At this period when there are revolutionary changes taking place in the world, dispassionate analysis is so important to the President and to himself. We live in a period where conditions change rapidly. We need to know not just what world leaders are saying*

> *but what they mean. We need to have their statements put into a background context. That is why CIA's analysis is so important.*[2]

While DCI James Schlesinger only spent a relatively short time at CIA, he thought so highly of Bruce Clarke and OSR's analysis that before he left in July 1973 to become secretary of defense, he asked Clarke to be his intelligence representative to the MBFR talks in Vienna. With DCI Colby's approval, Clarke took the job on loan to DoD for an extended assignment that lasted until he returned to CIA in early 1979 to work with DCI Turner.

High Praise

Turner lavished praise on CIA's military analysis. In his book *Secrecy and Democracy*, Turner not only commended the "enormous skill" of CIA analysts, but he pointed out that the DCI's only boss is the president and that CIA's customers are everywhere in Washington, including the White House and the Departments of Defense, State, and Treasury. Turner stated that CIA has no obvious policy bias, and he lamented the fact that DIA and the military services failed to measure up to the competition. He blamed this on an insufficient number of competent people and an inability to withstand Defense Department pressures to support DoD policies. Turner added:

> *It would hardly be fair not to point out that the budgetary process in our country virtually forces the military to use intelligence to overstate the threats they must be ready to counter. If each military service does not exaggerate the threat, it is almost certain to have its budget cut. The issues of military intelligence estimates, then, are issues of bureaucratic budget politics as well as of intelligence. Largely as a result of these pressures, I found DIA's participation in the NIE process less than useful.*[3]

DCI Robert Gates also has expressed strong admiration for CIA's military analysis during the Cold War period. In his book *From the Shadows*, Gates wrote:

> *The great continuing strength and success of the analysts of CIA and the intelligence community was in describing with amazing accuracy from the late 1960s until the Soviet collapse the actual military strength and capabilities of the Soviet Union... we located and counted with precision the number of deployed aircraft, tanks, ships, and strategic weapons. And the numbers and capabilities could be relied upon, with confidence, by the Executive Branch (including the Defense Department), the Congress, and our allies, both in arms control negotiations and in military planning.*

Gates added:

> *Perhaps the intelligence community's greatest contribution was that during the last half of the Cold War there were no significant strategic surprises—no more "bomber gaps" or "missile gaps" as in the 1950s. Further, our detailed knowledge of Soviet forces and capabilities after the middle 1960s made it virtually impossible for the Soviets to bluff us, and this helped prevent miscalculations and misunderstandings that could have destroyed the world...for a quarter century, American Presidents and the Congress negotiated and made decisions with confidence in our knowledge of the adversary's actual military strength—a confidence that was justified.*[4]

Gates also commented on a short version of this OSR history published in CIA's journal, *Studies in Intelligence*:

> *It is a great little history of an organization and its analysts that really made a difference for the country. My stint at the SEC lasted only three weeks before Stan Turner drafted me to his office. But I spent nearly two years in the SALT Support Staff and so saw firsthand the caliber of analysts and leaders you write about. I always thought Bruce Clarke was the finest leader I worked for at CIA. We could have used him far better at headquarters in those years than at MBFR. . .The names you cite in the history brought back a lot of fond memories.*[5]

Lost Legacy

Several former senior managers of military analysis in CIA, including Bruce Clarke, Richard Kerr, Rae Huffstutler, and Noel Firth, have expressed their fears that in the aftermath of the collapse of the Soviet Union, OSR's legacy of a strong independent capability to do military analysis in CIA for policymakers has been lost. They also worry that the president and Congress will be ill-served if they are forced to rely on DoD as the primary source of intelligence on foreign military threats and conflicts, particularly those involving US forces. US defense budgets and weapons programs are based heavily on such intelligence inputs, and it is only natural for the Pentagon to want a budget that assures a strong deterrence against future conflicts and US superiority if a conflict arises. But overestimating foreign military threats and capabilities and not taking into account political and economic constraints on foreign military intentions can result in poor policy decisions that upset fragile military balances and risk igniting wider regional conflicts.

Clarke, commenting on Firth and Noren's book *Soviet Defense Spending,* made the following statement:

> *The President and his advisors need effectively to formulate the foreign and military policies that assure the well-being of the Republic in the era of weapons of mass destruction. Because of the budgetary implications involved, the Congress has an equal claim for substantive, informed military intelligence analysis and judgment. And the Agency's experience throughout the decades since 1947 fully demonstrates that military intelligence analysis at the national level, where the Director of Central Intelligence is critically responsible for the needs of the President and Congress, is too important to be left to the military.*
>
> *Time and again, as I made my rounds to the White House, to the Office of the Secretary of Defense, and to the Hill as Director of Strategic Research, it was repeatedly impressed on me that, next to the agency's demonstrated professional and substantive intelligence experience in military analysis, the most important quality we possessed was our organizational freedom from departmen-*

> *tal budgetary concerns. None of our users were worried that we were likely to be skewing the analysis in favor of this or that U.S. weapons system.*[6]

In the same book, Firth added:

> *I am convinced—having spent more than thirty years closely observing the dynamics of the CIA relationship with the military in producing foreign military assessments—that the agency's participation in the process has saved the U.S. taxpayer many billions of dollars, contributed significantly to maintaining reasonable stability in the world balance of nuclear forces, and made nuclear arms control agreements possible.*[7]

Huffstutler has worried that with the end of the Cold War, national security customers, including the president and Congress, are much less interested in strategic military threats. The issues that concern them are international terrorism, narcotics trafficking, political unrest, and local conflicts. He believes that military analysis in CIA has become largely redundant. He points out that CIA now relies heavily on DIA and the military services for military order of battle, and that the CIA defense-costing effort on Russia and China no longer exists and would be difficult to reconstruct. As a result, the Pentagon now dominates the field of assessing foreign military threats to US national security interests.[8]

Kerr goes even further in expressing his concerns. In a recent interview for this study, Kerr expressed his firm belief that CIA lost its way during the past 30 years.[9] He stated that the agency has essentially become a current intelligence organization that no longer does in-depth research and analysis. Instead, it focuses on providing current intelligence support to national security policymakers and to military counterterrorism operations. Kerr also believes that the Defense Department now dominates the Intelligence Community. All directors of national intelligence (DNIs) from 2002 to 2017 were military officers, and the Pentagon now owns the major overhead intelligence collection programs. Finally, Kerr also believes that the CIA no longer has a strong independent voice to challenge DoD on national security policy issues such as Iraq and Afghanistan, where US military forces are involved.

Kerr believes the decline began in late 1981 when the DI was reorganized under DCI Casey along regional lines to better support national security policymakers, including the NSC, State, and the Pentagon. He believes the Agency got too close to policymakers and became too focused on current intelligence reporting at the expense of in-depth research and foreign intelligence analysis. According to Kerr, the next big step in the decline came in the early 1990s with the Iraq invasion of Kuwait and the collapse of the Soviet Union.

Kerr said that before Operation Desert Storm, CIA had never regarded intelligence support to US military operations as one of its key missions. This was left to DIA, the military intelligence services, and the combatant commands. But this changed after Desert Storm, when CIA was accused of not providing enough intelligence support to military operations. Kerr said that in response, the position of associate deputy DCI for military support was created. After the collapse of the Soviet Union, CIA began reducing the number of military analyst positions, and the defense budget costing efforts for both Russia and China were ending. CIA was also no longer able to maintain its own robust military databases for most countries; it increasingly relied on DIA, NSA, and NPIC for military order-of-battle information. This close relationship began to crumble in 1996 when DCI John Deutch transferred NPIC to the Pentagon and ended CIA's role in the satellite imagery collection program.

Kerr stated that the final big change came in 2001, after the 9/11 terrorist attacks. CIA began to focus on counterterrorism as a major mission, and it provided extensive intelligence support to the US invasions of Afghanistan and Iraq. These events increased the need for current intelligence reporting and support for counterterrorist and military operations, and in-depth research and analysis suffered still more. Kerr added that when the DNI position was created in 2005 to better manage the entire IC, the ultimate result was a procession of military DNIs who would further transform the CIA into a policy support organization. Finally, Kerr sees the new Mission Manager reorganization as the final step in the transformation of CIA from its roots as an independent intelligence organization dedicated to doing in-depth analysis of foreign threats to US national security interests to an organization that focuses on current intelligence. This is because he believes the mission managers are focused on providing ongoing intelligence support to national security policymakers at the expense of in-depth analysis of key foreign threats and the stability of major regional strategic military alliances.

Many former OSR analysts and managers would undoubtedly agree with Kerr to varying degrees. Some, the author of this study included, might add that the Pentagon now has so much influence over the IC that it would be politically difficult, if not impossible, for the CIA to do independent analytic assessments of the Iraq and Afghanistan conflicts or of the Russian and Chinese strategic military threats to US national security interests without the support of DoD. Without reliable, basic military intelligence support from DoD, it would not be feasible for CIA to undertake its own in-depth, competitive research and analysis on regional military conflicts involving US forces that would represent an effective challenge to the Pentagon's own assessments.

In the last interview that Bruce Clarke had with the CIA history staff in 2004, he commented that the real work of a national intelligence organization is to create new knowledge, and that this is accomplished by doing in-depth research and production. Whether CIA needs to have the capability to do independent strategic military analysis in the current global and political environment is well beyond the scope of this history, but it would be an interesting topic for future study of key US national security interests and mechanisms.[10]

❖ ❖ ❖

Endnotes

1. Richard Helms, "To the People of the Office of Strategic Research," 1 July 1972. www.cia.gov.

2. Henry Kissinger, address to CIA on its 25th Anniversary, 18 September 1992, www.cia.gov.

3. Stansfield Turner, *Secrecy and Democracy*, 238 and 248.

4. Robert Gates, *From the Shadows*, 526.

5. Robert D. Vickers, Jr., "CIA's Office of Strategic Research: A Brief History," in CIA, CSI, *Studies in Intelligence* 62, No. 1 (Unclassified articles from March 2018), 39-47.

6. Firth and Noren, *Soviet Defense Spending*, 206.

7. Ibid., 206.
8. Rae Huffstutler, interviewed by Robert Vickers, 6 November 2015.
9. Richard Kerr, interviewed by Robert Vickers, 10 October 2017.
10. Bruce Clarke, interviewed by Donald Steury, 12 January 2004.

❖ ❖ ❖

Appendix

DCIs: 1946–93

RAdm. Sidney William Souers, USNR	Jan.–June 1946
Lt. Gen. Hoyt Sanford Vandenberg, USA (AAF)	June 1946–May 1947
RAdm. Roscoe Henry Hillenkoetter, USN	May 1947–Oct. 1950
Gen. Walter Bedell Smith, USA	Oct. 1950–Feb. 1953
Allen Welsh Dulles	Feb. 1953–Nov. 1961
John Alex McCone	Nov. 1961–April 1965
VAdm. William Francis Raborn Jr., USN (ret)	April 1965–30 June 1966
Richard McGarrah Helms	June 1966–Feb. 1973
James Rodney Schlesinger	Feb. 1973–July 1973
William Egan Colby	Sept. 1973–Jan. 1976
George Herbert Walker Bush	Jan. 1976–Jan. 1977
Adm. Stansfield Turner	March 1977–Jan. 1981
William Joseph Casey	Jan. 1981–Jan. 1987
William Hedgcock Webster	May 1987–Aug. 1991
Robert Michael Gates	Nov. 1991–Jan. 1993

DDIs: 1952–89

Loftus Becker	Jan. 1952–April 1953
Robert Amory Jr.	May 1953–March 1962
Ray S. Cline	April 1962–Jan. 1966
R. Jack Smith	Jan. 1966–May 1971
Edward W. Proctor	May 1971–June 1976
Sayre Stevens	June 1976–Oct. 1977
Robert R. Bowie (D/NFAC)*	Oct–Aug. 1979
Bruce C. Clarke Jr. (D/NFAC)*	Aug. 1979–April 1981
John N. McMahon (D/NFAC)*	April 1981–Jan. 1982
Robert Michael Gates	Jan. 1982–April 1986
Richard J. Kerr	April 1986–March 1989

*The Directorate of Intelligence was named the National Foreign Assessment Center during this period.

DDS&Ts: 1963–95

Albert D. "Bud" Wheelon	Aug. 1963–Sept. 1966
Carl E. Duckett, Acting DDS&T Actual DDS&T	Sept. 1966–April 1967 April 1967-June 1976
Leslie C. Dirks	June 1976–July 1982
R. Evans Hineman	July 1982–Sept1989

Index

A

B

C

D

E

F

G

H

I

J

K

L

M

N

O

P

Q

R

S

T

V

W

Y

www.ingramcontent.com/pod-product-compliance
Lightning Source LLC
Chambersburg PA
CBHW080403270326
41927CB00015B/3331
* 9 7 8 1 7 8 2 6 6 9 4 3 2 *